641.692

GW00372282

THE NEW FISH COOKBOOK

THE NEW FISH COOKBOOK

Janet Horsley

PIATKUS

Copyright © Janet Horsley 1986

First published in 1986
by Judy Piatkus (Publishers) Ltd, London

British Library Cataloguing in Publication Data

Horsley, Janet
    The new fish cookbook.
    1. Cookery (Fish)
    I. Title
    641.6'92   TX747

    ISBN 0–86188–500–7

Edited by Susan Fleming
Illustrated and designed by Paul Saunders

Typeset by Phoenix Photosetting, Chatham
Printed and bound by Mackays of Chatham Ltd., Kent

For A.C.M.P., with love and thanks

CONTENTS

INTRODUCTION

My childhood memories of fish are probably typical of a good many people's, in that we were limited to a once-a-week meal of fried fish and chips – home-made of course! – and crab salads on special occasions. It wasn't that we didn't like fish; just that it always seemed to take second place to meat. One reason for this was that the fish-monger only visited our small town twice a week. The cod, plaice and haddock which he sold from his van were wonderfully fresh, but by no stretch of the imagination could the choice be described as adventurous. I only began to appreciate the wide variety of shapes, colours, flavours and textures which can be found on a fish-monger's slab when I went to live in a city with a small but lively fish market. There, under the watchful eye of a friendly fishmonger, I began to experiment with monkfish, bream, squid, garfish and mussels.

The great variety of fish now available is obviously one reason why sales are increasing, but there is another reason: that of health. In recent years much has been written about our eating habits, and we have been bombarded with information about what we should and should not be eating. While some of that advice does not have the full support of the medical profession, almost everyone agrees that our consumption of fat should be reduced, in particular the saturated fat found in meat and dairy products. Fish happens to be low in fat, and even the oilier varieties such as mackerel, herring and sardines are considered to be a healthy alternative to meat, for not only is the fat unsaturated but it is also rich in essential fatty acids.

I try to ensure that the other ingredients I use are wholesome too, and in my recipes wholewheat flour and brown rice are substituted for white varieties, unrefined and cold pressed oils for chemically treated ones, yoghurt for cream, fresh vegetables for canned, and herbs and other natural seasonings are used instead of synthetic flavourings.

Whatever the reason for buying fish, I hope that this book will encourage everyone to be a little more daring when it comes to selecting fish – for it must not be assumed that the most expensive varieties are always the best. Certainly a poached salmon lends a certain air of distinction to a meal, but in itself it won't make that meal memorable. It is much better to use your eyes and nose and to choose fish that both looks and smells fresh, if necessary substituting one variety for another.

Although the old-fashioned fishmonger, selling his wares from dripping boxes piled high with wet fish, is a less familiar sight these days, the number of retail outlets selling fresh seafood has increased. Supermarkets, in particular, have some excellent fish counters and I find it hard to resist displays of gleaming, colourful fish attractively arranged on trays of crushed ice. Delicacies such as smoked trout, scallops and red mullet are relatively new arrivals, and I am sure that they, along with many other interesting and unusual visitors to the fish stalls, have helped to stimulate our imagination and make us more appreciative of the excellent fish to be found in our rivers and off our coastlines.

Unless otherwise stated, all recipes included in this book will serve four people.

A GUIDE TO THE MARKET PLACE

Shopping for fish can be both exciting and frustrating, as the availability of different varieties is very unpredictable. Weather and the seasons apart, there seems to be no rhyme or reason why one day the fishmonger's slab should be brimming over with countless fish, while a few days later, usually when you have invited family or friends to dinner and have a specific recipe in mind, the choice is minimal and the quality dubious. Haddock, plaice, trout, golden cutlets, kippers and prawns can generally be relied upon, but one is less certain of finding cod, herrings, mackerel, coley, halibut, sole, hake, whiting, Finnan haddock, gurnard, garfish, mullet, mussels, conger eel, squid, octopus and cuttlefish.

Living, as I do, in a city whose population comprises numerous nationalities and cultures, I notice the fishmongers becoming more cosmopolitan. They are happy to cater for the needs of the Chinese, West Indian, African, Asian and East European communities, and snappers, salt cod and St Peter's fish lie side by side with the more familiar cod, haddock and plaice. Provided that they are not too busy, I have found fishmongers more than willing to give advice on how to prepare and cook these unusual varieties, most of which are well worth buying. My only reservation is that the more exotic fish, which are usually found in warmer waters than our own, arrive deep frozen. Sometimes they are sold in the frozen state, but generally they are thawed out first and unscrupulous fishmongers sometimes try to pass them off as fresh fish.

If frozen fish are thawed out badly they tend to be unpleasantly watery and lacking in texture, so avoid any that have lost their natural lustre and look dull and flabby. This is not to say that frozen fish doesn't have its uses; in some cases it can be a better buy than fresh fish, particularly when the quality of the fresh fish is dubious or when you want to put it straight into your own freezer. It is not worth trying to freeze fish at home, as domestic freezers simply aren't powerful enough. The large ice crystals which inevitably form can spoil both the texture and the flavour of the fish.

It is necessary to be a discerning buyer when selecting any fresh produce but never more so than when buying fish. These days, with modern refrigerated containers and an efficient transport network, there is really no excuse for the sale of bad fish. In any case it is not too difficult to tell fish that is 'off', the smell usually being sufficient warning in itself. The real problem today is in spotting the difference between fish which is fresh and that which is stale and way past its prime. Really fresh fish should look as if it has just been caught; the body will be taut and firm, the skin moist and slippery, the colour bright and iridescent, the eyes clear and bulging, the gills red and the smell fresh and pleasant. If the fish has already been filleted the flakes should be moist and translucent. As always there are exceptions to the rule, in this case skate and rays. Their flesh contains a chemical known as urea which controls the level of body fluids, and when the fish dies the urea is gradually broken down, giving off a faint smell of ammonia. A slight whiff of ammonia is therefore a sign of freshness, but don't be too disappointed

if your skate smells of nothing but fish for many fish-mongers deliberately keep their skate a day or so to allow the smell to dissipate. The skate itself is none the worse for this delay; in fact, if anything, it is improved for as the urea is broken down the flesh becomes more tender.

With a little practice it becomes fairly easy to identify good quality fish, but actually making one's purchases is not always quite so straightforward. The matter becomes complicated when the particular variety of fish you want is not in very good shape and compares unfav-ourably with others on offer. There is no problem if all you want to do is poach, fry or grill the fish and serve it perhaps with a sauce, for in this case almost any white fish will do and you can therefore buy a fresh sample of a similar variety. The real dilemma arises when you have decided to make a special dish and the fish you need is either unavailable or not worth buying. You can, of course, abandon the first recipe, choose another type of

fish, rush home, sift through your cookery books to find another recipe, check the contents of your food cupboard against the list of ingredients and go out shopping once again for the missing items – but more often than not this simply isn't practical or desirable. A better way round the problem is to make yourself familiar with the types of fish generally on sale so that you are confident about substituting one variety for another should the need arise. Being able to put names to the different fish is a great help, particularly if you can identify those which belong to the same family, but it is also useful to be knowledgeable about their flavour and texture and whether or not they are oily. You should find the follow-ing classification helpful.

SOFT-TEXTURED WHITE FISH

This category of fish has been described as the mainstay of the fishing industry for it includes the three most popular varieties – cod, haddock and plaice. All have lean white flesh which is easy to digest but, because of their soft texture, care must be taken not to overcook them. Naturally some are better flavoured than others, a fact which tends to be reflected in the price. Depending on the size, and whether the fish is whole, filleted or cut into steaks, this category of fish can be poached, baked, grilled, shallow-fried, battered and deep-fried, braised and used in soups. For the purposes of substituting one fish for another I have divided this category into two groups:

Round fish

This group includes cod, haddock, hake, grey mullet, whiting, coley and ling. Cod, haddock and hake have the best flavour and texture and are in a class of their own. The usefulness of the other fish should not be underesti-

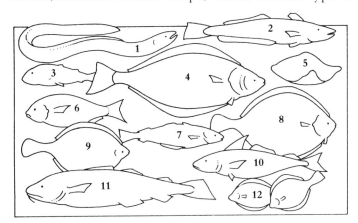

White Fish
1 conger eel   2 hake   3 red mullet   4 halibut   5 skate wing
6 sea bream   7 whiting   8 turbot   9 plaice   10 haddock   11 cod
12 dabs

mated; being fairly cheap they are ideal for making fish pies, fish cakes and curries and for giving body to stocks and soups.

Flat fish

Plaice, lemon sole and dabs are included here. Plaice is marginally better, but all are of good quality and can be substituted one for another. However, don't make the mistake of confusing lemon sole with Dover sole. Although they have a similar name they have little else in common.

FIRM-TEXTURED WHITE FISH

Included in this category are Dover sole, turbot, monkfish and halibut, all fish of the highest quality and so much in demand with the catering industry that they are rare visitors to the fishmonger's stall. Their firm white flesh makes them suitable for almost any cooking

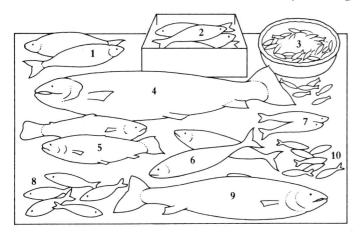

Oily Fish and Freshwater Fish
1 and **2** herrings   **3** whitebait   **4** salmon   **5** trout   **6** mackerel
7 smelts   **8** sardines   **9** salmon trout   **10** sprats

method and some cooks have even suggested that they can be treated as if they were meat. Certainly I have substituted monkfish for veal on a number of occasions with great success. All the fish included in this category can be poached, grilled, shallow-fried, battered and deep-fried, baked, braised, casseroled and used to great advantage in soups and stews. The firm texture of the fish means that it can be slightly overcooked or kept waiting without coming to too much harm – a fact that hasn't been overlooked by chefs and restaurateurs. For the purposes of substitution I have divided the category into three groups:

Large fish sold as steaks and fillets

This includes monkfish, halibut, turbot, large Dover sole and brill, John Dory, dogfish and skate. Obviously the cooking times for, say, a halibut steak and a fillet of Dover sole will be different, and this must be taken into account when a substitution is made.

Small fish sold and cooked whole

Small brill and Dover sole, red mullet, gurnard and bream are included here. They are an ideal size for one person and can be grilled, baked, stuffed or cooked *en papillote*.

Miscellaneous fish

Conger eel and garfish are both eel-shaped and, depending on size, may be sold whole or in steaks. Although of similar size, shape and texture the conger eel has a much stronger flavour which is not to everyone's liking. Both fish tend to be bony, particularly towards the tail end.

OILY FISH

This category includes tuna fish, mackerel, herrings, sardines, sprats, whitebait and smelts. With the exception

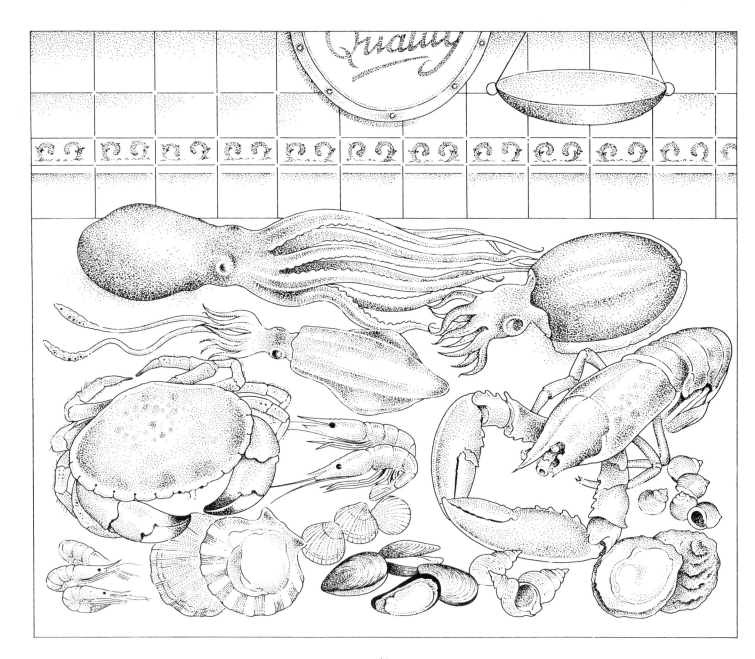

of tuna all the oily fish have a fairly soft texture and are generally small enough to be sold and cooked whole. Freshness is essential when buying this category of fish for the oils soon become rancid and the flavour unpleasant. I think that oily fish are at their best grilled or fried, but they can also be poached, particularly in court-bouillon made with wine or cider, which helps to counteract their oiliness. Traditionally they are also served with sharp sauces based on mustard, gooseberries, rhubarb, citrus fruits, watercress and sorrel. They can be substituted one for another, depending to a large extent on size although tuna fish, being richly flavoured and firm fleshed, is best used in specific recipes.

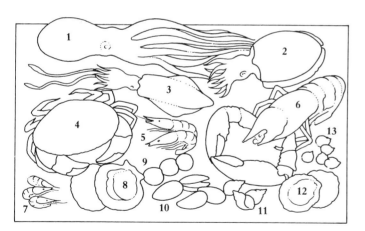

Cephalopods and Shellfish
1 octopus 2 cuttlefish 3 squid 4 crab 5 prawns 6 lobsters
7 shrimps 8 scallops 9 cockles 10 mussels 11 whelks
12 oysters 13 winkles

CEPHALOPODS

Octopus, cuttlefish and squid are all cephalopods, and have their heads located between a sac-like body and an array of tentacles. They are believed to be the most intelligent of all molluscs but this fact has done nothing to improve their popularity. Many people find them repulsive and it is hardly surprising that we have been slow to appreciate their gastronomic value, for the tangled mass of slippery bodies and tentacles so often seen at the fishmonger's is not a particularly appealing sight. Yet underneath the ugly exterior is a milky white flesh which looks neither frightening nor repulsive.

Cephalopods are best appreciated in the Mediterranean and the north-western Pacific, but there are signs that we in north-western Europe are beginning to be a little less squeamish. I welcome the initiative of some fishmongers who try to make their wares look more attractive. Instead of having to fish around in a wooden box brimming over with flabby bodies, you can choose your cephalopod, often already skinned, from neat displays beautifully arranged on crushed ice.

All cephalopods are sweetest and most tender when young. Tiny squid and cuttlefish, measuring less than 7.5cm/3 inches, can be battered and deep-fried whole. Octopus are by far the toughest and are best gently stewed for an hour or so; this is also an excellent way to cook full-sized squid or cuttlefish. Many recipes call for the black/brown ink or sepia which is located in the silvery ink sacs. Used by cooks and artists alike with dramatic effect, it is by no means essential and many delicious dishes can be prepared without it. Some fishmongers remove the ink sacs when cleaning the fish and even if they are left intact they are not always easy to find. Until you are happy about handling cephalopods I would suggest that you only use the sac-like body and the tentacles – leave rummaging for the ink sac to those more familiar with the creature's anatomy. While the famous Italian dishes of *seppie al nero* and *risotto nero* are certainly eye-catching, not everyone finds black an appetising or appealing colour.

SHELLFISH

Overfishing and pollution have taken their toll of shellfish stocks but hopefully the situation will soon improve as more and more varieties are being intensively farmed. To some degree the price of shellfish reflects its quality and scarcity with lobsters being the most expensive, followed by oysters, scallops, clams, Dublin Bay prawns, crabs, prawns, shrimps, mussels, cockles, winkles and whelks. With so many shellfish being frozen these days it is particularly important to buy from a fishmonger who has a high turnover to ensure that your purchases are fresh and sweet-tasting. The high price of most shellfish precludes them from being eaten in large quantities, and they are generally served as starters or used in small amounts to flavour soups, soufflés, salads, curries, pies and quiches. In some cases shrimps can be used instead of prawns and clams and cockles instead of mussels but generally one is better sticking to the recipe.

PRESERVED FISH

'If this weather holds I'm a dunner. Fish won't keep, y'know. I had a case o' fresh whiting in yesterday and the missus fainted. Went clean away. That's the fish-trade. See y'money go bad under your eyes.'
H.E. Bates, *Country Tales*
(Reader's Union Publishers, 1938)

The need to preserve fish was much greater in the days before refrigeration, particularly as the Christian calendar specified as many as twelve meatless days a month. As a result, numerous cottage industries grew up around our fishing villages and ports, thriving on the nationwide demand for pickled, salted, dried and smoked fish. Nowadays far fewer fish are preserved and (apart from rollmops) pickled, salted and dried fish have largely disappeared from our shops. Smoked fish on the other hand have become very popular, although they are very different from those sold a century ago. Now the smoking process is much lighter, with the sole purpose of flavouring the fish rather than preserving it. Some products are still smoked by traditional methods using hardwood shavings while others, known in the trade as painted ladies, are artificially dyed and flavoured. It is not difficult to spot these imposters for their colour is rather gaudy, as one might expect.

The range of smoked fish is extensive and includes kippers, Finnan haddock, Arbroath smokies, buckling, bloaters, smoked salmon, smoked trout and smoked cod's roe. It is possible to substitute one smoked fish for another provided that you ask yourself the following questions:

Is the fish to be served whole? If the answer is yes then it is important to use a fish of similar shape and size to that suggested in the recipe.

Is the texture and flavour of the fish essential to the success of the dish? For example, smoked haddock is an essential ingredient when making a kedgeree, while a pâté can be made, with confidence, using almost any smoked fish.

FRESHWATER FISH

Today almost all the freshwater fish found on the fishmonger's slab will have spent their lives at a fish farm.

Their flavour may not be quite as good as that of river fish but, on the other hand, there is less danger of them tasting muddy. Freshwater fish tend to be bony and the flesh may be dry, Trout, salmon trout and salmon are the most common freshwater fish, and may be poached, grilled, baked and stuffed. Trout are lighter in colour and texture and are less oily than the salmon. The salmon trout combines the best features of both and can be used as a substitute for either fish.

HOW MUCH TO BUY

It is difficult to stipulate precise quantities as the needs of individuals and families vary enormously, but as a general guide it can be assumed that one person will need:

150–175g/5–6 oz fillets
175–200g/6–7 oz steaks
225g/8 oz small whole fish or portion of large whole fish

And it bears repeating that, unless otherwise stipulated, all the recipes in the book serve four people.

STORING FISH

Keep the fish cool and as soon as possible rinse well under cold running water. Pat dry and wrap loosely in absorbent kitchen paper, then place in foil or a plastic bag. Store it in the coldest part of the refrigerator, away from foods which may absorb the smell, until needed. Fish is best eaten on the day of purchase, but if you must store it overnight, remove the gills and viscera before putting in the refrigerator.

Shellfish deteriorate more quickly than other varieties of fish and my advice is to use them straightaway, particularly prawns which have already been defrosted.

CLEANING AND PREPARING FISH

Fishmongers are generally more than happy to scale, decapitate, clean, skin and fillet fish but they are less than willing to do anything out of the ordinary, and if you want your fish gutting through the gills or need the backbone removing for stuffing it is necessary to do it at home.

Cleaning and preparing fish is not a particularly gruesome or difficult task and I tend to clean all my fish at home as a matter of course. The advantages are threefold. Firstly, fish is best prepared as close to cooking as possible so that it does not have time to dry out and lose flavour; secondly the fish's head, tail and bones are too useful for making stock to be left behind at the fishmonger's; and finally one is able to prepare the fish exactly to one's requirements.

SCALING

Many varieties of fish are covered in iridescent scales which are usually so small that they do not need to be removed. The principal exceptions are the scales of the sea bream and grey and red mullet, which are coarse and unpleasant to eat. To scale a fish you need to use a blunt blade or the reverse edge of a kitchen knife; anything sharper may damage or tear the delicate skin. Take hold of the fish by the tail and scrape the blade down towards the head. This will dislodge the scales and, more likely than not, send them flying in all directions. As a precaution cover all adjacent foodstuffs or scale the fish under cold running water.

GUTTING

Flat fish

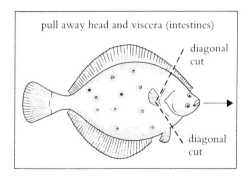

pull away head and viscera (intestines)

diagonal cut

diagonal cut

Remove the head with two diagonal cuts; most of the viscera (intestines) will come away too. Clean out the cavity, rinse well and pat dry.

Round fish
a) Through the gills

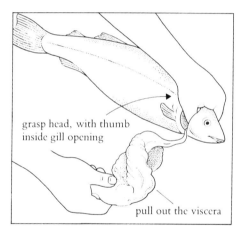

grasp head, with thumb inside gill opening

pull out the viscera

Pull the gill flaps open, with your thumb inside the gill opening. Hook a finger inside and hoik out the red gills, pulling as much of the viscera with them as possible. Reach into the cavity and clean out any residue. Rinse carefully and pat dry.

Cleaning fish through the gills is not as easy as it sounds, particularly when dealing with small fish, but it is a neat way of preparing a fish which is to be served whole or stuffed. If care isn't taken, however, the fish can become rather mauled in appearance, thus defeating the whole object of the exercise. Please don't let me put you off trying to gut fish through the gills; practice makes perfect, after all, but if you don't master the art don't despair. In the end if may be better to accept defeat gracefully and to make a neat and tidy job of gutting the fish in the more conventional way through the belly.

b) Through the belly

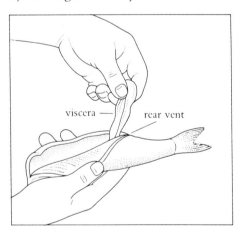

Cut the head off below the gill flaps and slit open the belly down to the rear vent. Remove the viscera and any traces of blood, particularly any lying along the backbone. Rinse well under cold water and pat dry.

If the head is to be left on remove the gills and then slit open the belly from just behind the head to the rear vent. Remove the viscera, rinse and pat dry.

SKINNING
Flat fish

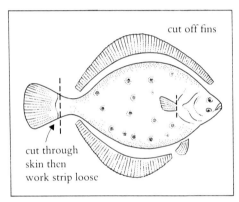

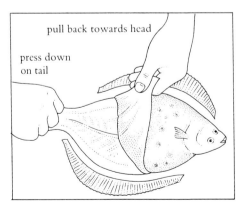

Most flat fish are skinned whole. Lay the fish, dark side uppermost, on the work surface, with the tail towards you. Trim off the fins. Cut through the dark skin where it joins the tail and carefully work a 2.5-cm/1-inch strip loose. Press down firmly on the tail using a tea cloth or piece of kitchen towel to give a better grip and then take hold of the loose skin with the other hand. Pull the skin decisively and firmly towards the head; the skin should come away in one piece. The white skin is usually left on flat fish except when preparing Dover sole.

Round fish
Round fish can also be skinned whole. First cut the skin along the length of the belly and the backbone and proceed to skin as if it were a flat fish. However, it is more common, and easier, to skin round fish after they have been filleted.

Lay the fillets, skin side down, on a chopping board and work about 1.25-cm/½-inch of skin loose at the tail end. Press down firmly on the loose skin, with one hand. Take hold of a sharp knife in the other hand, place the blade between the flesh and skin and, with short diagonal strokes, separate the fillet from the skin.

FILLETING

Flat fish

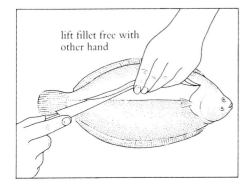

lift fillet free with other hand

Lay the fish, skinned or unskinned, thick or dark side up, on a chopping board and remove the fins. Then cut along the backbone from head to tail. Insert the tip of a sharp flexible knife into the slit at the thickest part of the fish, and slowly work down and along one side of the fish with knife and fingers, keeping the knife as close to the bone as possible until the fillet is free. Do not rip the flesh. Turn the fish round and remove the second fillet. Now turn the fish over and do the same on the other side. When you have finished you will have four fillets.

Round fish

Round fish only have two fillets but they are removed from the bone in exactly the same way as those taken from a flat fish. Put the fish on a chopping board on its side and make a deep cut along the backbone. Insert the tip of the knife and work across

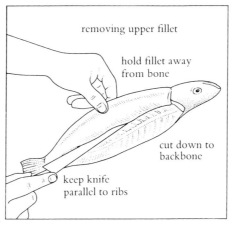

removing upper fillet

hold fillet away from bone

cut down to backbone

keep knife parallel to ribs

the bone, in short diagonal strokes, until the fillet is free. Turn the fish over and repeat to remove the fillet from the other side.

BONING

As well as being able to fillet round fish it is also helpful to know how to bone them without actually cutting them into fillets. There are three different methods depending on the type of fish being used.

A trimmed and gutted fish

If the fish is soft fleshed and is already

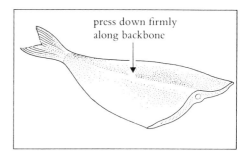

press down firmly along backbone

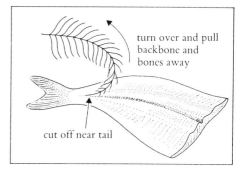

turn over and pull backbone and bones away

cut off near tail

decapitated and gutted, the simplest method is to extend the belly opening down to the tail. Then gently open the fish out and place it on a chopping board, skin side uppermost, and press down firmly along the backbone. Turn the fish over and tug gently at the backbone – it should come away quite easily bringing with it most of the other smaller bones. Cut or snap it off at the tail end.

If the head is to be left on, the fish can be boned through the belly or the back.

A whole fish gutted through the belly

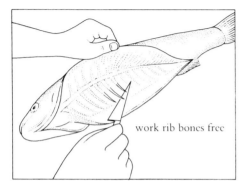

work rib bones free

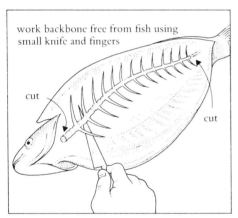

work backbone free from fish using small knife and fingers

cut

cut

If the belly has already been opened for cleaning, extend the opening down to the tail. Open the fish as wide as possible without tearing the skin. Using the fingertips, and perhaps a small knife, work the rib bones free. When both sides are free snip through the backbone where it joins the head and joins tail. Work the backbone free and gently pull it and the rib cage away from the flesh. Remove the gills if necessary. Rinse and pat dry.

A whole fish from the back

This is an attractive alternative to the above method, and one which is particularly useful if you intend stuffing the fish. Slit the fish open along the backbone and work down each side of the rib cage with a sharp knife to free the bones. When they are

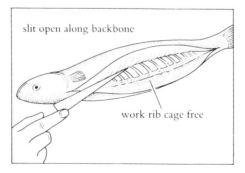

slit open along backbone

work rib cage free

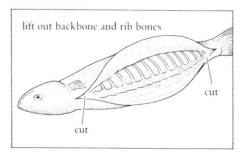

lift out backbone and rib bones

cut

cut

worked free, snip through the backbone where it joins the head and tail, and lift it out. All the small rib bones should come away with it. Remove the viscera and the gills. Rinse carefully and pat dry.

CEPHALOPODS

Cephalopod means 'head-footed' and refers to the fact that the creatures' heads are located between their bodies and their feet or tentacles. Octopuses have eight tentacles while cuttlefish and squid have eight short ones and two longer ones. They can all be prepared for cooking in no more time than it takes to gut any other fish but unfamiliarity makes the task a much more daunting proposition. Unfortunately the instructions found in many books are not always very useful for the novice. Advice such as 'remove the beak, eyes and internal organs' may be helpful to those already familiar with the basic anatomy of a cephalopod, but I well remember when I tackled my first squid; it took me at least five minutes to locate the eyes, and if I actually removed the beak it was more by luck than skill!

I most admit that preparing cephalopods is not one of my favourite pastimes, but I have perfected a simple method for each type which is quick, straightforward and relatively clean. Prepared squid can sometimes be found at good fish shops.

Squid

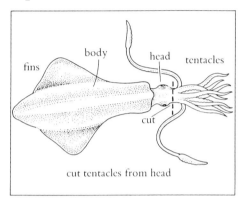

cut tentacles from head

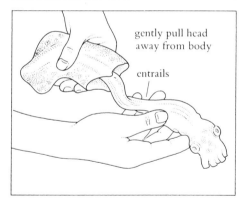

gently pull head away from body

entrails

First locate the tentacles, the sac-like body with its two fins and the narrow head lying between the tentacles and the body. Then cut off the tentacles just below where they are attached to the head and place on one side. Take

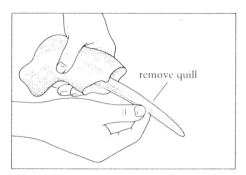

remove quill

hold of the head in one hand and the body in the other and pull the two sections gently apart. The viscera, including the ink sac, will come away with the head and can be discarded.

The sac-like body will be empty now, except for the quill and a little mucus membrane. Locate the end of the transparent quill, grasp it by the tip and pull it free from the body and discard. Rinse the body under cold running water and carefully pull out the mucus with the fingers.

Some squid are sold still shrouded in their veil-like translucent skin, irregularly mottled with pinkish grey patches. It covers the body and is easily peeled away.

Remove the skin from the two fins and pull them from the body. They come away quite easily and should be placed with the tentacles. Rinse well and pat dry. The squid's tentacles, fins and sac-like body are now ready for use (see final drawing).

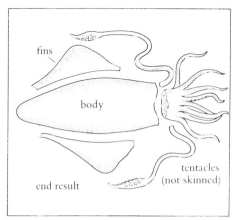

fins

body

tentacles (not skinned)

end result

Cuttlefish

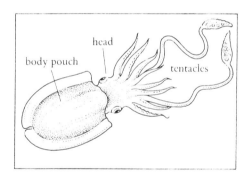

head

body pouch

tentacles

Cuttlefish are prepared in much the same way as squid except that the large white cuttlebone is more difficult to remove. Hold the body pouch in one hand and grasp the head in the other and pull the two sections gently apart. The viscera, including the silvery ink sac, will come away with the head and can be discarded.

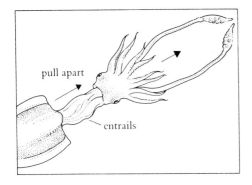

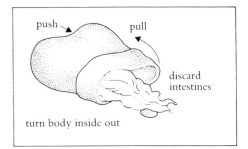

to make a cut through the body sac running the length of the cuttlebone. Once removed, rinse the empty body sac and remove any remaining mucus and sand. Peel off the skin, rinse well and pat dry. The cuttlefish is now ready for use.

Octopus

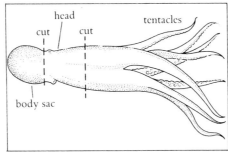

Identify the tentacles, the sac-like body and the narrow head running between the two. Remove the head by cutting off the tentacles and the sac-like body. Discard the head and retain the rest.

Cut off and discard the suckers and any loose skin from the tentacles, including the ends.

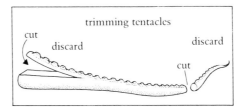

Ease the body inside out, cutting the inners away from the fleshy bag as you do so. Discard the viscera. Rinse the sac-like body and the tentacles under cold running water. Pull away the remaining dark skin, blanching it if it proves stubborn. The octopus bag and tentacles are now ready for use.

SHELLFISH

Oysters

To open an oyster shell you need a steady hand and equal amounts of care and brute force. The task is made easier by using a proper shellfish knife which has a short stout blade with a protective shield just below the handle. However, any strong bladed kitchen knife will do, provided that extra care is taken.

The fishmonger will often open oysters for you, but this is only practical if you are going to eat them there and then, for inside each shell is a small amount of salty liquid which is

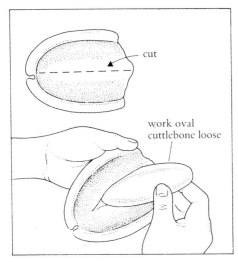

Locate the tip of the cuttlebone with your fingers and cut through the flesh of the body pouch at this point until the blade meets the bone. Grasp the cuttlebone between the fingers and gently work it loose. If it is particularly stubborn it may be necessary

held in high regard by connoisseurs and is supposed to be downed in one gulp with the oyster itself.

Always work with the flat side of the shell uppermost and keep the oyster horizontal so as not to spill any of the liquor. Insert the blade under the hinge and press it deep into the oyster. Twist the knife sharply until the two shells are forced apart. Free the oyster and check that there is no extraneous material in the shell – it is more likely to harbour sand and grit than a precious pearl! The oyster is now ready for use.

Scallops

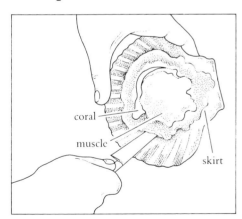

coral
muscle
skirt

Scallops always seem a little easier to open than oysters. They can be opened with a sharp stout knife, as if they were oysters, or baked, hollow shell down, for a few minutes in a moderate oven until the shells begin to gape open.

Gently lever the two shells apart and slip a knife under the dingy grey-brown membrane or skirt surrounding the white scallop muscle. Separate the edible white meat and orangy-pink coral and discard the skirt and black intestinal thread. Rinse gently and pat dry. The scallop is now ready for use.

Mussels

Like all fresh shellfish, mussels should be eaten on the day they are purchased.

To clean them, place them in a large container of salted water and sprinkle a handful of oatmeal or flour over the top. Leave to stand for 1–2 hours. Discard any that float to the surface. Scrape off any barnacles and scrub each mussel under cold running

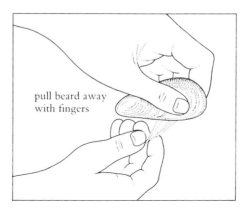

pull beard away with fingers

water. Pull away the stringy beard which protrudes from the concave side of the shell. Rinse again and discard those that are damaged, open or feel very heavy.

To open the shells, put into a large pan containing a little water or wine. (Don't try to cook too many at a time.) Cover and bring to the boil. Simmer for 2–4 minutes, shaking the pan frequently, until most of the mussels have opened. Remove from the pan and strain off the liquid. Discard any mussels that have not opened. The mussels are now ready for use.

Lobster and crawfish

Lay the cooked lobster on its back and snap off its eight legs, as close to the body as possible. Break each leg in two and extract the slivers of meat concealed inside. Break off the claws, crack them open and remove the meat.

To open the body, place it on a chopping board, belly down, and cut through the shell – using a serrated knife – starting at the head and working down towards the tail. Work carefully, splitting the lobster completely in two. Pull the two halves apart to reveal the meat. In the female lobster the bright red coral is easily identifiable and should be removed and put to one side. Next,

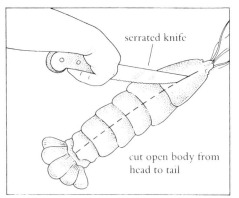

serrated knife

cut open body from
head to tail

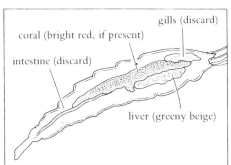

coral (bright red, if present)

gills (discard)

intestine (discard)

liver (greeny beige)

remove and discard the dark thread-like intestinal canal which runs down the middle of the white meat at the tail end. Then work the white meat free at the tail end and gently pull it away from the shell, breaking it off where it joins the grey-brown gills in the middle of the body. The soft greeny-beige tomally or liver is edible and should be removed. Discard the rest of the lobster.

The coral, if present, the white meat and liver are now ready for use.

Crabs

To remove the meat from a cooked crab, lay it on its back and break off the claws and legs. Put these to one side until later.

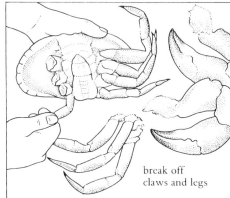

break off
claws and legs

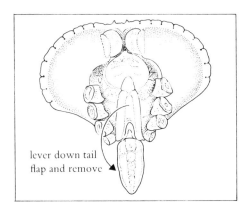

lever down tail
flap and remove

Push back and remove the bony pointed tail flap and insert the tip of a strong knife into the back of the crab's underbelly, where the hard

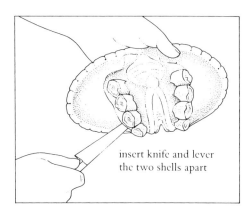

insert knife and lever
the two shells apart

shell meets the undershell. Lever the two shells apart – it may be necessary to insert your thumb into the gap to prise them apart.

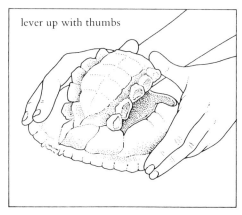

lever up with thumbs

Take hold of the large top shell and remove the stomach-sac and mouth, located just below the crab's eyes. Scoop out the brown meat and put into a small bowl.

spoon out brown meat

remove stomach
sac and mouth

meat. Open the legs and claws, remove the slivers of white meat and put into a separate bowl.

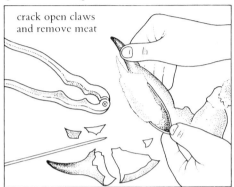

crack open claws
and remove meat

remove gills

That is the easy part. Now one has to settle down with a fine skewer or knitting needle and a pair of nut-crackers to extract the rest of the

Remove the grey-brown gills (also known as dead men's fingers) from the underbelly of the crab and

discard. Cut the underbelly in half and scrape the white meat from all the nooks and crannies. The white and brown crab meat are now ready for use and can be piled back into the top shell.

COOKING FISH

Fish deserves to be called a convenience food, for it is both quick and easy to prepare. It can be poached, grilled, fried, braised or baked but never, never boiled. Boiling is one of the chief reasons for dry tasteless fish, but overcooking can also be to blame, and should be avoided whichever method is used.

Fish requires little cooking and must not be left unattended for long. It needs to be tested regularly so that it can be removed from the heat the moment it is tender. Even then it will carry on cooking and in order that it can be taken to the table immediately while still moist and succulent, all sauces, vegetables and garnishes should be prepared beforehand. The firmer textured fish such as Dover sole, halibut, turbot and monkfish will tolerate some delay, but you should never keep haddock, cod or plaice waiting, for their soft texture quickly becomes as characterless as soggy white bread.

Although there are many delicious recipes for fish soups, stews and braised dishes, it is generally accepted that the best way to cook a really fresh fish is as simply as possible. However, a dish of poached, grilled, steamed or fried fish, no matter how fresh, is generally improved by the addition of a sauce, provided that the sauce neither attempts to mask nor compete with the fish itself. Recipes for sauces admirably suited to being served with fish can be found on pages 46–53.

STEAMING

The fundamental principle behind steaming any food is to keep it away from the boiling liquid generating the steam. For this reason most steamers are designed to sit on top of another pan, but there are also smaller, collapsible steamers on the market which open out like a concertina and fit into the bottom of a pan, supporting the food above the water level. I also take the precaution of protecting the fish from the steam itself by wrapping it in a piece of foil *en papillote* and placing this loose parcel inside the steamer. Not only does this make serving much easier – there is little risk of breaking the fish as it is lifted out of the pan – but it also seals in all the fish's goodness, flavour and juices. Don't worry if you don't have a steamer, it is easy enough to improvise with a metal colander fitted with a foil lid or better still, with two metal plates.

Steaming is an excellent method of cooking fish, in particular thin fillets of such fish as plaice, dabs, lemon sole, Dover sole and brill.

Steaming filleted fish
Lightly brush a sheet of foil with melted butter or oil and lay the fillets on top, making sure that the pieces do not overlap one another. Season well and sprinkle with lemon juice. You may like to add a sprig or two of fresh herbs such as tarragon, thyme, parsley or chives. Wrap the foil around the fish to form a loose but secure parcel. Place in the bottom of the steamer or metal colander and cover with a tight fitting lid. Stand over boiling water, making sure that the parcel is well above the water level. Cook until the fish is tender: the precise time will vary depending on the thickness of the fish and the type of steamer used. Thin fillets take between 8–15 minutes,

while thicker pieces, up to 2.5-cm/1-inch thick, take between 20–25 minutes. I don't steam anything thicker than this as it takes too long, and the results aren't as good as you might expect.

Steaming between two plates

Steaming food between two metal plates may sound a little Heath Robinsonish, but it is extremely effective. Grease or oil the plates to prevent the fish sticking and then arrange the fillets on top of one of them (again they must not overlap). Season to taste and sprinkle with lemon juice and, if desired, a few herbs. Cover with the other plate. The plates must be of similar size so that the seal between the two is fairly good. Stand over a pan of boiling water and cook until the fish is tender.

POACHING

Presentation and flavouring apart, the key to successful poaching is the use of first-class ingredients and precise timing. It is also vital to ensure that the fish is *not* cooked in boiling water or stock; in fact the temperature of the poaching liquid should not exceed 88° C/190° F. However, it is not necessary to go to the trouble of testing the temperature with a thermometer; simply bring the liquid to a slow boil, reduce the heat and let it cool slightly before adding the fish – the surface of the liquid should be quivering rather than bubbling. The only time fish is actually boiled is when making stock or broth for a soup; then the trimmings are boiled hard so that every last drop of flavour is given up to the liquid. Poaching, on the other hand, keeps the delicate flavour trapped inside the fish and ensures that the flakes stay moist and intact. Fish can be poached in plain salted water but the flavour is improved by using court-bouillon or fish stock (see pages 39–41).

Almost any type of fish can be poached, although those with a firm texture are the most suitable as they tolerate a certain amount of overcooking. Timing is all important and it is essential that you watch the pan carefully, testing the fish every now and then so that it is not left in the hot liquid a moment longer than necessary. It is difficult to give precise cooking times as so much depends on the size and thickness of the fish, but here are some guidelines:

thin fillets and shellfish	3–5 minutes
medium fillets, steaks and cutlets, small whole fish weighing 225–450g/½–1 lb	5–8 minutes
thick fillets, steaks and cutlets, whole fish weighing 450–900g/1–2 lbs	8–12 minutes
whole fish 1–2 kg/2–4½ lbs	10–20 minutes
whole fish 2–3 kg/4½–7 lbs	20–30 minutes

The size and shape of the fish also determines the type of cooking vessel to be used. Traditionally fish was poached in a fish kettle, a large deep oval pan fitted with a two-handled trivet on which the fish was placed. Such pans are ideal for dealing with large whole fish but are of little practical use to the modern family which tends to be smaller and less formal than that of a generation ago. Should you need to cook a whole salmon for a special

Right: Scarborough Pie (page 59) and Hake Provençal (page 84).

occasion, a large roasting tin can be used, but it would be better to hire a fish kettle from a reputable kitchen shop so as to eliminate all risk of breaking the fish while lifting it in and out of the pan. When dealing with smaller whole fish, fillets, steaks or cutlets, any pan can be used provided that the fish fits snugly in the bottom and that a minimum amount of liquid is required to cover the fish.

Poaching a whole fish

This is an ideal method of preparing a whole round fish such as salmon or salmon trout which is to be served hot. Presentation is all important, as nothing looks worse than a ragged, torn and broken fish.

Trim the fish but do not scale. Clean and discard the gills and rinse carefully under cold running water. Pat dry with absorbent paper. To help retain the shape of the fish during cooking I usually tie it up loosely with twine or soft string as if it were a parcel. Place the trussed fish on the rack of a fish kettle and lower into the pan. Barely cover with cold, strained court-bouillon. Lift the rack holding the fish out of the pan and keep aside while bringing the court-bouillon to a very slow boil. Reduce the heat until the surface is hardly moving then gently lower in the fish. Cover and poach until tender, using the cooking times given on the previous page as a guideline.

When the fish is cooked lift from the pan, drain, and slide onto a serving dish. Remove the string. Slit the skin from head to tail along the back and belly and gently pull it away on the exposed side. Make a deep cut, down to the bone, along the length of the fillet and, using a flexible blunt knife, work the flesh free of the bone. Divide into portions and serve. When all the upper fillet has been eaten, cut through the exposed backbone where it joins the tail and gently lift it up. Cut it again where it joins the head and discard. Now the lower fillet is boneless and ready to serve.

The soak poaching method

Useful for cooking any whole fish which is to be served cold.

Place the cleaned and trimmed fish on a rack in the bottom of a pan or fish kettle. Just cover with cold court-bouillon and bring to a slow boil. Poach for 2–3 minutes, then remove from the heat and leave to cool. When completely cold remove from the liquid, drain and serve. Any fish, no matter what its size, will emerge from the soak tender, moist and succulent.

Jug poaching

An excellent trouble-free method of cooking and reheating some types of smoked fish. The beauty of this

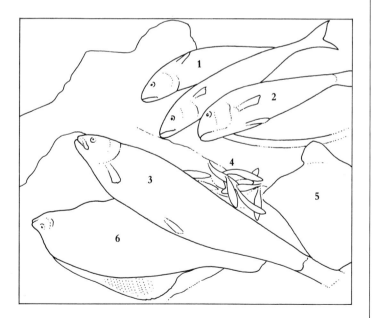

1 mackerel 2 red mullet 3 salmon 4 whitebait 5 skate 6 plaice

method is that neither the kitchen nor any piece of equipment is tainted by the smell of the fish which, in the case of kippers, can be rather overpowering.

Stand the fish, tail uppermost, in a tall jug and cover with boiling water or court-bouillon so that just the inedible tail protrudes. Leave to stand for 5–10 minutes, depending on size and thickness of the fish, until heated through. Take hold of the fish's tail and pull out of the jug. Drain and pat dry with absorbent paper. Serve hot or cold.

GRILLING

Grilling is one of the nicest ways of cooking fish. Not only is it quick but, to quote Marcel Boulestin in *The Best of Boulestin* (ed. Elvia and Maurice Firuski, Heinemann, 1952): 'it seems somehow to bring out the sea flavour and increase the quality of the flesh'. The flavour of the fish can be enhanced further by cooking it with herbs, by marinating and basting it with an aromatic oil or by cooking it over hot charcoal embers as in barbecuing.

Most fish can be grilled, provided that they are not too large. The most usual varieties are small mackerel, herrings, red mullet, gurnard, trout, turbot and sole. Larger fish can be grilled if they are first cut into fillets and steaks. All need to be basted frequently during cooking, lean white fish more than oilier varieties, to prevent the flesh scorching and drying out. For this reason many cooks prefer to leave the skin on the fish as it offers some protection against the fierce heat. Very small fish can be protected further by being wrapped in vine or lettuce leaves.

The principles of grilling fish are the same as for meat. The fish is first painted with oil or butter and then put under a hot grill for a minute or two before the heat is reduced and the cooking continued at a slower pace. The skin of the fish is usually crisped up under the hot grill but try to resist the temptation to turn the fish too often and always handle it carefully using tongs, a fish slice, palette knife or a double-sided, two-handled grill specifically designed for the purpose.

Whole round fish, weighing more than 175g/6 oz, should be scored with two or three deep cuts on both sides to allow the heat to penetrate the thicker, fleshier parts and to ensure even cooking. Whole flat fish such as sole and turbot, on the other hand, are cut lengthways along the backbone. Cooking times obviously vary from fish to fish, but as a rule fillets take less time and require a less fierce heat than, say, a whole plump trout or herring. Always keep a watchful eye on the grill while cooking as a minute or two can make all the difference between a perfectly cooked fish and a dry overcooked one. Cook until the flesh is opaque and comes away from the bone.

Grilling a whole fish

Clean and scale the fish if necessary and score any thick, fleshy parts to ensure even cooking. To add flavour to the fish you can stuff the body cavity with fresh chopped herbs or rub some into the scored flesh. Brush with oil or melted butter and season. Lay the fish on an oiled rack and place under a hot grill. Cook, turning once, until tender. Baste with oil or pan juices as and when necessary during cooking.

BARBECUING

Whole small- or medium-sized fish such as red mullet, herrings, sardines and trout and firm-fleshed varieties such as halibut, monkfish and tuna are excellent choices for the barbecue. Whole fish can simply be brushed with oil before being cooked, but steaks, cutlets and fillets are best marinated first in a mixture of oil, lemon juice, herbs and seasoning. Steaks and cutlets can be cooked whole while fillets are better chopped into chunks, threaded onto skewers and barbecued with a selection of vegetables. Baste the fish frequently with oil or the marinade mixture during cooking.

FRYING

Marcella Hazan quotes Brillat-Savarin in her authoritative book, *The Classic Italian Cookbook* (Papermac, 1981), by defining perfectly fried food as ' "surprised" in hot fat, which quickly imprisons its natural flavour and texture intact within a crisp, light crust'. To ensure good results the fat must be very hot, the food and coating of good quality and, perhaps most important of all, the golden parcels must be eaten straightaway while piping hot.

Small- to medium-sized whole white fish, fillets and steaks are all excellent deep- and shallow-fried. However, because of the searing heat involved, it is necessary to protect the fish in some way before immersing it in the hot fat. The traditional coatings of flour, oatmeal, egg and breadcrumbs and batter not only offer the fish protection but also make them easier to handle, improve their appearance and flavour and stop them absorbing too much oil. The fish should not be more than 2.5-cm/1-inch thick, otherwise they will not cook through in the time it takes for the coating to become crisp and golden brown.

Coatings for frying
Seasoned flour or oatmeal
If the flesh of the fish is dry, moisten with a little milk or water so that the coating will adhere. Put a handful of flour or oatmeal on a plate and season to taste. Dip both sides of the fish in the flour, shaking off any surplus before putting aside. Leave to dry for several minutes before cooking.

Egg and breadcrumbs
Two beaten eggs and 100g/4 oz dried breadcrumbs are usually sufficient to coat four fillets. Use either home-baked dried breadcrumbs or bought 'golden' crumbs. First sprinkle the fish with seasoned flour, shaking off any surplus before dipping into the beaten egg. Put the breadcrumbs on a plate and press both sides of each fillet gently onto them so that they adhere well. Leave the coated fillets aside to dry and firm up for 15–20 minutes before cooking.

Batter
Use a batter coating for deep fried fish.

BATTER

50g/2 oz wholewheat flour
50g/2 oz unbleached white flour
a pinch of salt (optional)
150ml/¼ pint water
2 tablespoons sunflower oil
1 egg white

Mix the two flours together in a bowl and add the salt, if using it. Make a well in the centre and pour in the water. Gradually work into the flour, mixing well until smooth. Add the oil and beat vigorously until the surface is covered in bubbles. Whisk the egg white until peaked and fold into the mixture. If using a blender or food processor put the flours, salt (if using it), water and oil into the goblet and process until smooth. Spoon into a bowl. Whisk the egg white until stiff and peaked and then fold into the mixture. Dip the fish into the batter and then slide into the hot fat.

Deep-frying

The key to successful deep-frying lies to a large degree in the choice and temperature of the cooking fat. The traditional ones are lard and clarified dripping, but because of their saturated fat content, more people are switching to vegetable oils. Groundnut oil and corn oil are especially good choices as they both have high smoking points. Some cooks suggest using olive oil but I find it a little too strongly flavoured and prefer to use the lighter oils which allow the flavour of the food itself to come through. The fat needs to be heated to 180°–190° C/350°–375° F so that the coating is 'set' almost immediately, sealing in the fish's flavour and juices. The temperature can be tested with a thermometer or by dropping a small cube of bread into the hot fat. If it rises to the surface immediately and becomes golden brown in about 30 seconds the fat is ready.

Having heated the fat to the required temperature the fish, which has first been coated in seasoned flour, egg and breadcrumbs or batter, can be slipped into the pan, but don't add too much at any one time or the temperature of the fat will drop significantly. As many kitchen accidents occur as a result of chip-pan fires and spillages of hot fat, never fill your pan more than half full. Cook for 5–10 minutes until golden brown, lift out and serve as soon as possible. Strain the oil into a clean bowl for use another time, but only use it for cooking fish as its flavour will have become tainted.

Shallow-frying

As the name suggests, shallow-frying involves the use of much less fat than deep-frying. In fact it should come no more than half way up the side of the fish being cooked which must then be turned at least once to ensure even browning and cooking. Small- and medium-sized whole fish such as trout, herring, plaice, sole or dabs can be shallow-fried as can most fish fillets and steaks provided that they are not too thick – 2.5 cm/1 inch is the maximum. Although the temperatures involved are not as high as when deep-frying it is still necessary to coat the fish in a protective coating of seasoned flour or egg and breadcrumbs. It is also important to clarify any butter beforehand to prevent it burning. This is not difficult to do – simply pour some melted butter through a sieve lined with damp muslin. Butter, vegetable oils or a mixture of the two are the most popular cooking fats. To test the temperature of the fat dip a corner of the coated fish into the pan and if it sizzles immediately the fat is hot enough, and you can proceed to cook the fish over a medium heat until tender. Cooking times will vary according to the type of fish and its thickness. Thin fillets may need as little as 3–5 minutes while thicker pieces may take between 10–15 minutes. Cook until the flesh is opaque and the coating crisp and golden brown.

Dry-pan frying

This method of frying fish is particularly useful for dealing with small oily fish such as herrings, sprats and whitebait. Heat a lightly oiled heavy frying pan and place the fish in the bottom – they must lie flat, in a single layer. Cook for 4–10 minutes (depending on size), turning occasionally until lightly browned and tender.

BAKING AND BRAISING

Baking and braising are methods of cooking whole fish, steaks and fillets in the oven. They are particularly useful when dealing with fish that are either too thick to grill or too large to fit into the poaching pan. It is important, however, to protect the fish from drying out in the oven and there are a number of ways of doing this: the fish can either be painted and basted with butter or oil, covered with a tight fitting lid, sealed *en papillote* inside a foil or greaseproof parcel, covered with a savoury topping, or braised – cooked in a covered dish on a bed of lightly sautéed vegetables moistened with a little wine, stock or water.

I find it most convenient to set the oven at gas mark 5 (190° C/375° F), irrespective of the size of the fish or the cooking method, and to vary the time taken. Thin fillets take between 8–15 minutes, thicker pieces 15–25 minutes, and whole fish 20–40 minutes.

Baking sur le plat

This is the simplest method of baking fish, and for it to be successful the fish must be very fresh and of good quality. Small- to medium-sized whole fish such as Dover sole, lemon sole, plaice, whiting and trout and most fillets and steaks can be cooked in this manner.

Clean the fish if necessary and lightly season before placing in the bottom of a shallow ovenproof dish. It should fit snugly with little room to spare. Pour over sufficient stock, water or lemon juice to cover the bottom of the dish to a depth of approximately 6 mm/¼ inch. Dot with butter. Bake uncovered, in a preheated oven, gas mark 5 (190° C/375° F), basting occasionally to prevent the fish drying out. Cook until the flesh is opaque.

Baking en papillote

Nicholas Soyer, grandson of the great chef Alexis Soyer, spent many years perfecting the paper-bag method of cooking, and indeed published a book extolling the virtues of his discovery. Cooking *en papillote* is now a fairly common practice and is particularly useful when dealing with fish. It is admirably suitable for cooking small and medium-sized whole fish, steaks and thick fillets.

Place the prepared fish on a piece of oiled or buttered foil or greaseproof paper. Season and lightly sprinkle with lemon juice. You may like to add a sprig or two of fresh herbs. Wrap up loosely but securely to form a parcel, thus sealing the fish's goodness, flavour and juices inside. Place on a baking tray and cook in a preheated oven, gas mark 5 (190° C/375° F), until tender. Many cooks put the parcels directly on to serving plates so that each diner has the pleasure and surprise of opening their own 'mystery' package. If opened in the kitchen, take care not to spill any of the cooking juices which should be poured over the fish before taking it to the table.

Baking au gratin

Gratin is the term given to a thin savoury topping which is sprinkled over foods and then browned in a hot oven or under a grill. The topping is usually made from soft breadcrumbs, seasoned to taste, and perhaps mixed with a few herbs and spices or grated cheese. It is dotted with butter before being baked. *Au gratin* dishes are commonly made with white fish fillets, whole small to medium flat fish which have first been boned, and shellfish.

Clean and skin the fish if necessary and place in the bottom of a buttered, shallow ovenproof dish. Season to taste. Pour over sufficient stock, wine or lemon juice to cover the bottom of the dish or cover the fish with a flavoursome béchamel sauce. Lightly cover with soft breadcrumbs and dot with butter. Bake, uncovered, in a preheated oven, gas mark 5 (190° C/375° F), until the fish is tender. If the topping hasn't browned in that time either raise the oven temperature to gas mark 8 (230° C/450° F) and cook for a further 5–10 minutes, or place under a hot grill.

Braising

Braising is a cooking method which combines the principles of baking and steaming. It is suitable for almost any type of white fish.

First sauté a selection of chopped vegetables – perhaps some onion, celery, leek, tomato and green pepper – in a little oil until they begin to soften. Then spoon the mixture into an attractive ovenproof dish and season to taste. Moisten with a little stock, lemon juice, wine or water (very little is needed if the dish contains a good proportion of tomatoes) and arrange the prepared fish on top. Cover with a tight fitting lid or foil and bake in a preheated oven, gas mark 5 (190° C/375° F), until the fish is tender. Baste the fish with the pan juices before taking to the table in the ovenproof dish.

FISH STOCKS, SOUPS AND STEWS

It is surprising that here in Britain, surrounded as we are by excellent fishing waters, there are so few traditional recipes for fish soups and stews. None compares with the great French *bouillabaisse*, the American chowder, or the Dutch *waterzootje*. Yet all our fish, with the exception of some of the oilier varieties such as herrings, mackerel and sprats, are used with great success in other countries.

The dividing line between a fish soup and a fish stew is sometimes rather blurred. Light bisques and creamy veloutés fall naturally into the first category, but what of the thick, chunky dishes that are the traditional fare of fishermen? White fish, crustaceans and cephalopods can be successfully cooked together in a large pot with chopped vegetables, herbs and other seasonings and eaten with whatever implement seems appropriate. In some households the broth is strained off and drunk as a soup before eating the remaining thick stew of roughly chopped fish and vegetables.

Soups and stews are, to my mind, the most delicious and satisfying ways of eating fish. They are surprisingly easy to prepare and can be made as plain or as elaborate as you wish. Light and delicate or strong and robust, smooth and creamy or roughly chopped and chunky; the variations are limitless. New and interesting flavours are created with each combination of fish.

Although almost any kind of fish, including small bony creatures which have no other culinary use, can be used to advantage in a soup or stew, it would take an exceptionally brave and imaginative cook to consider preparing such a dish from our fishmongers' usual offerings. The fish themselves are not to blame, for cod, haddock, plaice, dabs, sole, coley, whiting, smoked cutlets, mussels and prawns, are all extremely useful and versatile ingredients. The real problem lies in the way in which the fish are prepared for us, beautifully filleted, boned, cleaned, skinned and sliced with not a head, tail, bone or fin in sight.

Admittedly cleaning and gutting fish is not everyone's cup of tea but it is impossible to make good stock without the trimmings. If, as the French would have us believe, we are in the habit of cooking fish in plain salted water (this method is known as *poisson à l'anglais* across the Channel), there is little wonder that we have few recipes to compare with their fine repertoire of rich, aromatic soups and stews.

Court-bouillon and fish stocks

Court-bouillon is the name given to the liquid in which a fish is usually poached. It is used in preference to plain water because it enhances both the flavour and colour of the fish. Just enough is needed to cover the fish, the exact amount having as much to do with the size of the cooking pot as the size of the fish itself. Court-bouillon is usually made from water, wine vinegar or wine, chopped vegetables, herbs and spices. However, it can also be milk based. All the ingredients are simmered together for half an hour or so before being strained. It is always left to cool before being poured over the fish.

The liquid left over after the fish has been removed from the poaching pan is known as a fumet (many cooks refer to it simply as fish stock). The word literally means a scent or bouquet of fish. It has a much better flavour than a court-bouillon and is the basis of most fish soups and stews. If the fumet is reduced, by brisk boiling, from 850ml/1½ pints to 275ml/½ pint, it can be served as a sauce or used to enrich and flavour thick creamy sauces.

A fumet can be made in two ways; simply use the court-bouillon in which a piece of fish has been poached, or make it quickly and cheaply from 450g/1 lb or so of fish trimmings. It is always worth asking the fishmonger for some bones, heads, tails etc with your purchase of fish. Sometimes he will be glad to give them away, but even if you have to pay the amount will be small.

COURT-BOUILLON 1

This court-bouillon is excellent for poaching delicate white fish. For stronger flavoured fish, particularly freshwater eel, use red wine. In Normandy, cider takes the place of the wine.

1.2 litres/2 pints water
150ml/¼ pint dry white wine
1 onion, sliced
1 stick of celery, sliced
1 carrot, sliced
10 black peppercorns
2 sprigs of fresh parsley
2 sprigs of fresh thyme
2 sprigs of fresh fennel (optional)
1 bay leaf

Place all the ingredients in a large pan and simmer for about 30 minutes. Strain and leave to cool.

COURT-BOUILLON 2

A useful recipe for those occasions when there is no wine to spare. Red or white wine vinegar can be used.

1.2 litres/2 pints water
3 tbsps wine vinegar
1 onion, stuck with 3 cloves
1 leek, sliced
1 carrot, sliced
6 black peppercorns
2 sprigs of fresh parsley
1 sprig of fresh thyme
1 sprig of fresh tarragon (optional)
1 bay leaf

Cook as above.

COURT-BOUILLON 3

A good stock for poaching fish steaks and fillets. It is particularly good with white fish as it retains and even enhances its colour.

850ml/1½ pints water
275ml/½ pint milk
½ lemon, peeled and sliced

No preliminary cooking is needed. Place all the ingredients in a pan and poach the fish as directed in the recipe.

FUMET/FISH STOCK

**450g/1 lb fish trimmings
(try to include a fish's head or some bones, they give
body to the stock)
850ml/1½ pints water
150ml/¼ pint dry white wine
1 onion, sliced
1 carrot, sliced
10 black peppercorns
1 sprig of fresh parsley
1 sprig of fresh thyme
1 bay leaf**

Remove any pieces of gut or gills from the trimmings before placing them in a large pan with the other ingredients. Cover and bring to the boil. Skim and simmer gently for 30–40 minutes. Pass through a sieve, pushing through as much of the cooked vegetable mixture as you wish. If you intend to concentrate the fumet – to use it as an aspic, or if you need a clear stock – simply strain through a muslin-lined sieve and discard all the solids. The fumet can be stored in the fridge for several days and in a freezer for up to 3 months.

Fish soups and stews

The art of making successful fish soups and stews depends on much more than a good stock. The choice of fish is equally important and should include a selection from both the following categories:

whiting, coley, lemon sole, dabs, wrasse, grey mullet, gurnard.

haddock, cod, halibut, turbot, hake, monkfish, conger eel, red mullet, shellfish and cephalopods.

Fish from the first category are cooked in the stock until they quite literally disintegrate. Their bones etcetera are strained off, but not before the soup has been given a good deal of flavour and body. The fish in the second category are chopped into bite-sized pieces and cooked in the broth for a minimum length of time in order to retain their texture. A soup or stew should be judged not only by its flavour and colour but also by the texture of the roughly chopped fish served with it. The pieces should be tender but firm. This is easier to achieve if they are left in fairly large, bite-sized chunks. However, should you accidentally overcook the fish it is often better to purée it rather than serve it in tatters and shreds.

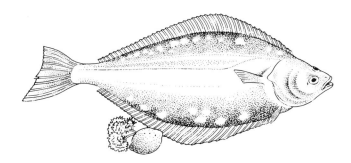

SOUPE DE POISSON

Here is a basic soup recipe which, in spite of its simplicity, is good enough to grace any table. The garnish of finely chopped tomato and parsley looks colourful against the whiteness of the fish and the golden broth. I like it best with hot crusty garlic bread but it is also delicious served with croûtons, parsley butter and *aïoli*, a garlicky mayonnaise from southern France.

Serves 4–6
1.7 litres/3 pints water
1 tbsp white wine vinegar
150ml/¼ pint dry white wine
1 onion, chopped
1 carrot, chopped
1 stick of celery, chopped
1 sprig of fresh parsley
1 sprig of fresh thyme
1 bay leaf
6 black peppercorns
1 whiting, cleaned
450g/1 lb fish trimmings
675g/1½ lbs assorted white fish
(cod, haddock, conger eel, skate, monkfish, halibut, hake)
a good pinch of saffron strands

FOR THE GARNISH
1 tomato, peeled and finely chopped
2 tbsps finely chopped fresh parsley

Put the water, wine vinegar, wine, chopped vegetables, herbs, peppercorns, the whiting and fish trimmings in a large pan. Clean the assorted fish if necessary before laying them on top of the other ingredients – they should be covered by the liquid ingredients. (If the assorted white fish do not fit comfortably into your pan, remove any skin and bones from the fish and simply add these to the pot. Cut the boned and skinned fish into bite-sized pieces and keep on one side, to be returned to the soup just before it is ready to be served. Then, instead of simply heating the fish through as directed in the recipe below, poach for 4–6 minutes until tender.)

Now back to the original recipe. Bring the contents of the pan to a slow boil. Reduce the heat, cover and poach for 5–6 minutes. Carefully lift the pieces of assorted fish from the pan and when cool enough to handle remove any skin and bones and cut into bite-sized pieces. Keep the pieces of fish to one side until needed and return the skin and bones to the pan. Bring to the boil again and cook for a further 10–15 minutes.

Pass the contents of the pan through a sieve into a bowl. Pound what is left of the whiting, fish trimmings and vegetables and push through the sieve. Rinse out the cooking pan and place the sieve over the top. Pour the fumet or stock from the bowl through the sieve and back into the pan. Press down on the contents of the sieve to extract all the stock. Discard the remains. Stir the saffron into the broth and bring to the boil. Cook for 10 minutes more. Just before the soup is to be served, add the bite-sized pieces of white fish and heat through. Ladle into individual bowls and sprinkle with chopped tomato and parsley.

Should you prefer a thicker soup, stir in a few nuts of *beurre manié*. This is a paste of butter and flour worked together until smooth. I use three parts butter to two parts flour. Thicken the stock when it is clear – that is after the soft fish and vegetables have been strained off but before the other white fish is added. Divide the *beurre manié* into small balls and stir them, one at a time, into the hot (but not boiling) stock. Wait until each knob has melted before adding another.

A soup can also be thickened and enriched with the addition of cream and egg yolk or by simply passing it through a vegetable mouli or by liquidising the ingredients in a food processor or blender.

ZUPPI DI PESCE

A puréed fish soup from Italy.

Serves 4–6

1kg/2–2¼ lbs assorted white fish
(red mullet, gurnard, conger eel, halibut, hake,
monkfish, haddock, cod, whiting)
1.5 litres/2½ pints fumet or fish stock (p. 41)
1–2 tbsps olive oil
2 onions, chopped
2 cloves of garlic, peeled and crushed
450g/1 lb ripe tomatoes, chopped
2 sprigs of fresh fennel (optional)
1 sprig of fresh parsley
1 sprig of fresh thyme
a good pinch of saffron strands
a good pinch of cayenne pepper
seasoning

Clean and trim the fish. Chop into large pieces, removing as many bones as possible, and keep aside. Place all the bones, skin and any heads and tails in a large pan with the stock. Bring to the boil, cover and simmer for 30 minutes. Strain and discard the solids.

Heat the oil in a large pan, add the onion and garlic, and sauté for 5–7 minutes. Add the pieces of white fish and the tomatoes and cook for a further 5 minutes. Add the

fumet/stock, just enough to cover, and the remaining ingredients. Bring to the boil, cover and simmer for 35 minutes.

Strain the soup and remove the herbs and any bones left in the fish. Then pass the vegetable and fish mixture through a vegetable mouli or rub through a coarse sieve and put back into the broth. Adjust the consistency and seasoning to taste. Heat through and serve with croûtons and grated Parmesan cheese.

This seems an appropriate place to mention bisques, those sophisticated soups which are the favourites of haute cuisine restaurants and expense-account dinners. Nowadays the term refers to thick, rich, creamy soups made primarily from shellfish, thickened with rice and flavoured with brandy. *Bisque d'homard* (lobster bisque) is perhaps one of the greatest of all soups and I suppose I shouldn't have been surprised to see it in cans on the supermarket shelves, ready to satisfy the appetites of modern gourmands at the turn of a can-opener. Not even idle curiosity has made me buy a can, I'd rather save myself for the real thing. Lobster makes such a rare appearance at my table, however, that I generally serve it whole rather than in a soup, no matter how delicious. Crab bisque is a different matter. It is equally rich and creamy but can be made at a fraction of the cost and the recipe on page 66 is well worth trying.

Creamed soups and bisques certainly get top marks for richness and refinement, but nonetheless my personal favourites are the fishermen's broths. They are more substantial than most soups yet not quite so filling as a meat-based stew. Served with hunks of fresh brown bread, and perhaps a salad to follow, they make an excellent meal for family and guests alike.

Almost every kind of fish caught by fishermen and

anglers found its way into the cooking pot at one time or another. Small bony ones were thrown in whole while larger meatier varieties were trimmed and chopped. It must be remembered that these soups-cum-stews were the daily fare of hard working fisherfolk and were relatively rough and ready affairs. For every spoonful of broth there must also have been a similar quantity of bones. I assume that with practice the fisherfolk mastered the knack of coping with such food, but unfortunately I don't yet seem to have done so. Sacrilege it may be, but I much prefer to eat my soups in the knowledge that they are free from bones. Perhaps if I ever get the chance to cook a *bourride* or *bouillabaisse* using the assortment of tiny silvery fish found in the markets of Mediterranean fishing towns I might change my mind. The size of the fish seems to be the critical factor. The bones of very small fish do not seem to present any problem and even I can crunch my way through a plate of crisp fried whitebait without batting an eye, but faced with anything larger I need a knife and fork, a fairly large plate and plenty of time!

Bouillabaisse is perhaps the most famous of all fishermen's stews. It is said to have originated in the coastal towns of southern France, in particular Marseilles. Certainly its heady aroma and bright colouring are typical of Provençal cooking. Thackeray has even written a sonnet called 'The Ballad of Bouillabaisse':

'This Bouillabaisse a noble dish is –
A sort of stew or broth or brew
Or hotch-potch of all sorts of fishes
That Greenwich never could outdo:
Green herbs, red peppers, mussels, saffern,
Soles, onion, garlic, roach and dace;
All these you eat at Terre's Tavern
In that one dish of Bouillabaisse.'

I am not sure where Terre's Tavern was situated but I have my doubts as to whether an authentic *bouillabaisse Marseillaise* ever included sole, roach or dace. More often than not the selection would depend upon what was available, either in the fisherman's nets or at the local market. A good *bouillabaisse* would generally contain some rascasse (a small bony fish, also called the scorpion fish and found mainly in Mediterranean waters), John Dory, monkfish, bream, red mullet, whiting, sea bass, gurnard, weever fish, wrasse, lobster and crab. The shellfish were invariably small, spiny and inedible. They were used simply to strengthen the broth. The only *bouillabaisse* actually to contain pieces of lobster and crab meat were those found in top-class restaurants.

BOUILLABAISSE

Traditionally *bouillabaisse* was eaten as two separate courses, the broth being drunk first with croûtons, followed by the more solid fishy parts served with a fiery red mayonnaise called *rouille*. Here is my version of this famous recipe, adapted to make full use of ingredients readily available in Britain.

Serves 4–6

FOR THE FUMET/FISH STOCK
1 gurnard, cleaned
450g/1 lb fish trimmings
1 whiting, cleaned
850ml/1½ pints water
150ml/¼ pint dry white wine
1 bay leaf
1 sprig of fresh parsley
1 sprig of fresh thyme
6 black peppercorns

THE REMAINING INGREDIENTS
**3–4 tbsps olive oil
1 onion, chopped
1 small Florence fennel bulb, chopped
3 beefsteak tomatoes, chopped
a good pinch of saffron strands
1.2kg/2½ lbs assorted white fish
(cod, haddock, conger eel, monkfish)
seasoning
2 tbsps finely chopped fresh parsley**

Put all the ingredients for the stock in a large pan and bring to the boil. Cover and simmer for 30 minutes. Pass through a sieve into a bowl, pushing through as much of the solid matter as you can.

Meanwhile heat the oil in another pan, add the onion and fennel and sauté for 5–7 minutes until they begin to soften. Add the tomatoes and cook for a further 5 minutes. Pour the fish stock over and stir in the saffron. Bring to the boil and simmer for 15–20 minutes. Trim the fish, removing any skin and bones, and cut into bite-sized pieces. Add the fish to the pan and bring to a slow boil. Reduce the heat and poach for 4–6 minutes until tender. Season to taste and sprinkle the parsley over the top.

SAUCE ROUILLE

**1 red chilli, seeds removed
3–4 cloves of garlic, peeled
1 slice of bread, crusts removed
1 egg yolk
150ml/¼ pint olive oil**

Finely chop the chilli and garlic. Soak the bread in water for 10 minutes then squeeze dry. Pound the three ingredients together until smooth or process in a food processor. Mix in the egg yolk thoroughly. Gradually add the oil, beating well after each addition, until the sauce becomes thick and creamy.

The fish soups and stews of the North Atlantic fishing ports are quite different to the colourful, heady dishes of the Mediterranean. Haddock features in many, as do potatoes and milk. In America they are known as chowders and in France *chaudrées*. The similarity between the two words is no coincidence. Originally French fishermen cooked their stews in large iron pans called *chaudières*. Each fishing boat had one, and inevitably they found their way, with French settlers, to the Eastern Seaboard where the word became anglicised. An excellent recipe for haddock chowder can be found on page 79.

SAUCES FOR FISH

Sauces need not be rich, complicated or fattening. Some are made with butter, some with milk, others with yoghurt or flour; eggs may be used too, and some sauces are made from concentrated fish stock. The flavour should complement the fish, and the sauce should be served in small amounts so that it does not mask or dominate the main dish. It is not always easy to indicate which fish is best accompanied by a particular sauce; more often than not the choice is too extensive to list and much depends on personal tastes and preferences. Tradition has it that the richer, egg-based sauces are served with high quality fish such as salmon, salmon trout, turbot and lobster, while sharper ones are used to accompany oilier fish such as herrings and mackerel. However, there are no hard and fast rules and it is much better and more interesting to follow your own inclinations.

Béchamel sauces

One of the basic sauces is made from a roux of butter and flour and is reputed to have been named after its creator, the Marquis de Béchamel, steward to Louis XIV. Béchamel sauces may not have the finesse of such sauces as hollandaise, *beurre blanc* and sauce Bercy but they are invaluable for adding interest and flavour to everyday dishes of haddock, plaice and cod. They can accompany almost any poached, baked, steamed, grilled or fried fish, and are useful for keeping fish moist and succulent while it is being baked in pies and *au gratin* dishes.

BÉCHAMEL SAUCE
(Thin pouring consistency)

425ml/¾ pint milk
2 slices of onion
2 slices of carrot
10 black peppercorns
1 bay leaf
1 sprig of fresh parsley
1 sprig of fresh thyme
15g/½ oz butter
1 tbsp sunflower oil
25g/1 oz unbleached white flour

Put the milk, onion, carrot, peppercorns, bay leaf, parsley and thyme in a saucepan and bring to the boil. Remove from the heat and leave to infuse for 20 minutes. Strain and reserve the flavoured milk. Heat the butter and oil together in a small pan, stir in the flour and cook gently until the mixture begins to bubble. Remove from the heat and gradually add the milk, stirring well after each addition. Return to the heat and bring to the boil, stirring continuously, until the sauce begins to thicken.

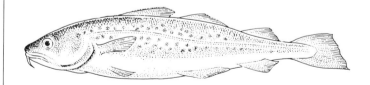

BASIC BÉCHAMEL SAUCE
(Coating consistency)

A true béchamel sauce is made with milk infused with vegetables and herbs, as in the recipe above, and the extra effort is well worthwhile as the flavour is greatly improved. However, time is sometimes at a premium and the following sauce is more basic.

15g/½ oz butter
1 tbsp sunflower oil
25g/1 oz unbleached white flour
275ml/½ pint milk
seasoning

Heat the butter and oil in a small pan, stir in the flour and cook for a minute or two until the mixture begins to bubble. Remove from the heat and gradually add the milk, stirring well after each addition. Return to the stove and bring to the boil, stirring frequently, until the sauce begins to thicken. Season to taste.

MUSTARD SAUCE

A particularly good sauce to serve with grilled mackerel and herring. Make 275ml/½ pint béchamel sauce, and just before serving stir in 1–2 teaspoons Dijon mustard.

CHEESE SAUCE

Make 275ml/½ pint béchamel sauce, and before serving stir in 50g/2 oz grated Cheddar cheese. Season to taste with freshly grated nutmeg.

PARSLEY SAUCE

An old favourite that goes with all types of poached, steamed, baked, grilled and fried fish. Make 275ml/½ pint béchamel sauce, and add 3–4 tablespoons chopped fresh parsley and several drops of lemon juice before serving.

CUCUMBER SAUCE

Serve with grilled, poached or baked salmon, salmon trout and trout.

15g/½ oz butter
15g/½ oz unbleached white flour
175ml/6 fl. oz milk
100g/4 oz cucumber, peeled and diced
seasoning

Melt the butter in a small saucepan, stir in the flour and cook gently until the mixture begins to bubble. Remove from the heat and gradually add the milk, stirring well after each addition. Return to the stove and bring to the boil, stirring well. Add the cucumber and spoon into a food processor or liquidiser and blend until smooth. Return to the pan and reheat. Thin down with a little more milk if necessary. Season to taste.

Velouté sauces

Ideal sauces to serve with fish which has been poached in court-bouillon, or to make when a little fish stock is available. They are made in the same way as béchamel sauce but all or half the milk is replaced by fish stock.

FISH VELOUTÉ
(Coating consistency)

15g/½ oz butter
1 tbsp sunflower oil
25g/1 oz unbleached white flour
150ml/¼ pint milk
150ml/¼ pint fish stock (p. 41)

Heat the butter and oil together in a small pan, stir in the flour and cook until the mixture begins to bubble. Remove from the heat and gradually add the milk and fish stock, stirring well after each addition. Return to the pan and bring to the boil, stirring all the time, until the sauce thickens.

SAUCE BERCY
(A white wine sauce)

A classic sauce which goes admirably well with all manner of grilled and fried fish.

1 shallot, finely chopped
3 tbsps dry white wine
275ml/½ pint fish velouté (see above)
1 level tbsp finely chopped fresh parsley

Put the shallot and wine in a small pan and bring to the boil. Cook until the wine is reduced by a half. Stir in the fish velouté and add the parsley.

SAUCE MORNAY

A good sauce for pouring over white fish and shellfish and baking au gratin.

Make 275ml/½ pint fish velouté (see above) and stir in 50g/2 oz grated Gruyère cheese and 1 tablespoon grated Parmesan cheese.

MUSHROOM SAUCE

25g/1 oz butter
100g/4 oz button mushrooms, chopped
25g/1 oz unbleached white flour
150ml/¼ pint milk
150ml/¼ pint fish stock (p. 41)
freshly grated nutmeg

Melt the butter in a pan, add the mushrooms and sauté for several minutes until their juices begin to run. Stir in the flour and cook for a minute or two over a moderate heat, stirring frequently. Remove from the heat and gradually add the milk and stock, stirring well after each addition. Return to the heat and bring to the boil, stirring well, until the sauce thickens. Season to taste with nutmeg.

Right: Filey's Good Friday Pie (page 69); photograph courtesy of the Potato Marketing Board.
Overleaf: Dressed Crab (page 65), Stuffed Mussels (page 103) and a langoustine.

To clarify butter

In a saucepan, heat the butter over a very low heat until it becomes as clear as olive oil, leaving a white deposit. Strain the clear liquid butter into a bowl. Use for dishes prepared *à la meunière*.

Butter sauces

BEURRE BLANC SAUCE

Especially good with any hot poached fish such as turbot, brill or salmon trout.

**juice of ½ lemon
1 tbsp white wine vinegar
1 shallot, finely chopped
50g/2 oz unsalted butter**

Put the lemon juice, wine vinegar and the shallot in a small pan and bring to the boil. Boil briskly until the liquid is reduced to a scant tablespoon. Strain and return to a clean pan, set over a low heat and gradually stir in the butter, a knob at a time, beating the mixture well as more and more butter is added. When all the butter has been used up the sauce should resemble shiny whipped cream.

BEURRE NOIR SAUCE

The classic sauce to serve with skate. Why the French decided to call it *beurre noir* is a mystery to me for 'black butter' is a totally inappropriate name for this golden, nutty brown sauce.

**50g/2 oz butter
1 tbsp white wine vinegar**

Melt the butter in a small pan and cook gently until it becomes golden brown. Pour it over the hot, cooked white fish. Then quickly tip the vinegar into the buttery pan – it should bubble and splutter. Pour over the fish and serve immediately while the butter is still sizzling.

Herb Butters

Savoury butters are a simple but effective way of adding the finishing touch to any plain cooked fish whether it be poached, steamed, baked, grilled or fried. They need to be firmed up in a refrigerator for an hour or so before being used. Herb butters can be made rather more in advance as they will keep for several days in the refrigerator and even longer, of course, in a freezer. Don't freeze garlic butter though as the flavour changes for the worse. Dot the savoury butter on top of the hot fish and take to the table immediately as the butter begins to melt. If you have the time try spreading the soft butter 6mm–1.25cm/¼–½ inch thick on greaseproof paper before chilling. When firm cut into small rounds or pats.

BEURRE MAÎTRE D'HÔTEL
(Parsley butter)

**50g/2 oz soft butter
1 tbsp finely chopped fresh parsley
a few drops of lemon juice
seasoning**

Put the butter in a small bowl and cream until soft. Stir in the remaining ingredients and season to taste. Shape and put in a cold place to firm up.

WATERCRESS BUTTER

Serve with grilled plaice, haddock or mackerel. Mix 1 tablespoon of finely chopped watercress into 50g/2 oz soft butter. Season to taste. Shape and chill.

GARLIC BUTTER

Mix 2–3 cloves of peeled and crushed garlic into 50g/2 oz soft butter. Season to taste. Shape and chill.

HERB BUTTER

Mix 1 tablespoon finely chopped shallot, 1 teaspoon chopped shallot and 1 teaspoon Dijon mustard into 50g/2 oz soft butter. Shape and chill.

MUSTARD BUTTER

Good with grilled mackerel and herring. Mix 1 finely chopped shallot and 1 teaspoon Dijon mustard into 50g/2 oz soft butter. Shape and chill.

MUSHROOM BUTTER

Mix 2–3 finely chopped mushrooms into 50g/2 oz soft butter. Season with a little freshly grated nutmeg. Shape and chill.

Egg sauces

These smooth, rich, creamy sauces are delicious served as an accompaniment to any poached, grilled or baked fish, especially lobster, turbot, sole and salmon, Serve egg-based sauces either warm or cold, but never hot.

HOLLANDAISE

Like all egg-based sauces hollandaise can separate out, but don't worry as it is not difficult to make provided you take your time and don't let the sauce become too hot.

2 tbsps white wine vinegar
2 tbsps lemon juice
10 black peppercorns
2 egg yolks
100g/4 oz unsalted butter   seasoning

Put the vinegar, lemon juice and peppercorns into a small pan and bring to the boil. Boil briskly until reduced to a scant tablespoon. Strain into a basin and leave to cool. Beat the egg yolks into the cool liquor and stand the basin in a pan of gently simmering water. Do not let the water boil. Whisk the egg mixture gently until it begins to thicken and then add a good knob of butter, whisking constantly until it has melted. Add another knob of butter and whisk again until that too has melted. Continue until all the butter has been used up and the sauce has the consistency of thick double cream. Pour into a warm sauceboat and serve.

If the sauce begins to curdle while it is being made, first beat in a tablespoon of very hot water. If that does not work put another egg yolk into a clean bowl. Place in a pan of warm water and gradually add the curdled mixture, stirring well after each addition.

MALTAISE SAUCE

An excellent sauce to serve with salmon trout. Replace the lemon juice of the hollandaise with the juice of a blood orange. Add the grated orange rind too.

GREEN PEPPERCORN SAUCE

Good with turbot and sole. Season the hollandaise with 1 teaspoon pounded green peppercorns.

SAUCE BÉARNAISE

A lightly flavoured hollandaise created by the chef to the French king, Henri IV.

1 shallot, finely chopped
150ml/¼ pint tarragon vinegar
3 egg yolks
100g/4 oz unsalted butter
2 tbsps finely chopped fresh tarragon
seasoning

Put the shallot and vinegar into a small pan and boil briskly until reduced to about 2 tablespoons. Strain and leave to cool. Then continue to make the sauce as if you are preparing a hollandaise. Stir in the tarragon and season to taste before serving.

HOLLANDAISE POISSON DE MER

Make as for hollandaise but use 2 tablespoons concentrated fish stock instead of the vinegar.

MAYONNAISE

Mayonnaise is one of the most popular summer sauces, enjoyed with salads and fish alike. It ought to be in everyone's repertoire for it really isn't difficult to make, particularly now that the electric blender has largely replaced the hand whisk, making the task so much quicker and easier. Being an egg-based sauce there is a danger that the mayonnaise may curdle during its making but provided that all the equipment and the ingredients (especially the eggs) are at room temperature, and the oil is added drop by drop, the risks are very low. However, should the worst happen a mayonnaise can be saved in much the same way as one would set about saving a curdled hollandaise (see page 50).

2 large egg yolks
1 tbsp white wine vinegar or lemon juice
275ml/½ pint olive or groundnut oil
seasoning

Put the egg yolks in a bowl or liquidiser and beat in 1 teaspoon vinegar or lemon juice. Then add the oil, drop by drop, beating well after each addition until the mixture begins to thicken. The oil can now be added in slightly larger amounts until it has all been absorbed. Add the remaining vinegar or lemon juice and season to taste.

MUSTARD MAYONNAISE

A delicious sauce to serve with shellfish. Beat 2 teaspoons Dijon mustard with the egg yolks and vinegar before adding the oil.

MAYONNAISE INDIENNE

Stir 1 teaspoon curry power with the egg yolks and vinegar before adding the oil.

TARTARE SAUCE

The classic sauce to serve with fried fish. Stir 1 teaspoon of each of the following – finely chopped chives, capers, parsley, gherkins and green olives – into 275ml/½ pint mayonnaise.

AÏOLI
(Garlic mayonnaise)

A marvellous sauce which originates in the Languedoc region of southern France where it is eaten with salt cod, *bouillabaisse*, squid and langoustines. Start as if to make a mayonnaise but mix 5 peeled and crushed cloves of garlic with the egg yolks and vinegar before adding the oil.

MUSHROOM AND YOGHURT SAUCE

A light, piquant sauce which goes well with poached and grilled white fish.

275ml/½ pint natural yoghurt
1 tbsp unbleached white flour
2 egg yolks
100g/4 oz button mushrooms, sliced
freshly grated nutmeg

Beat the yoghurt, flour and egg yolks together and pour into a pan. Add the mushrooms and cook over a low heat, stirring frequently until the sauce begins to thicken. Season to taste with nutmeg. Simmer gently for 3–5 minutes before pouring over the fish.

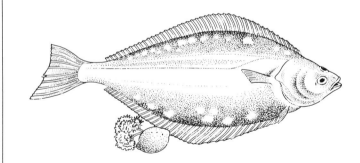

PRAWN SAUCE

A delicate sauce that can be served with any poached, steamed or baked white fish.

275ml/½ pint milk
2 eggs
100g/4 oz peeled prawns
seasoning

Beat the milk and eggs together and pour into a heavy pan. Add the prawns and cook gently, stirring all the time, over a very low heat until the sauce begins to thicken. Remove from the heat immediately and season to taste.

Strictly speaking, a sauce of this nature should be cooked in a bain-marie or in a basin set over a pan of gently simmering water and it should be stirred carefully and lovingly for 15–20 minutes until it thickens, but for speed and ease I prefer to cook it as described above. There is a risk that the sauce will become too hot and will separate out but if this does happen don't panic – simply pour the curdled mixture into a blender or food processor and whizz round once or twice. The sauce will become beautifully smooth and if anything better flavoured as the chopped prawns are more evenly distributed. However, don't over-process the sauce as the prawns must still be identifiable and not reduced to a purée. Reheat carefully over a very low heat.

A–Z OF FISH

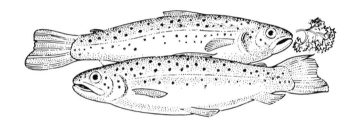

ARBROATH SMOKIES, *see* Smoked Fish

BLOATERS, *see* Smoked Fish

BRILL

Brill is a flat fish not readily available in Britain. It is not dissimilar to the turbot but is smaller and smooth skinned. The flesh is less firm and gelatinous than that of the turbot but it has a good flavour and can be used in recipes for turbot, halibut or sole. E.S. Dallas, writing under the pseudonym Kettner in the late nineteenth century, wrote, 'of all good fish, brill is the most odious, because it is used, either ignorantly or maliciously, to do duty for turbot. No doubt this is proof of its goodness; it would be impossible to pass off a bad fish for turbot.'

Brill is much smaller than turbot, weighing on average between 3–4kg/7–9 lbs, but it is still, by and large, too big to be cooked whole and is usually sold filleted. It can be poached, braised, fried, baked, cooked *au gratin* and in *matelotes*. It is traditionally served with hollandaise, *beurre noir* or with any butter sauce.

BRILL WITH EGGS AND SOURED CREAM

4 brill fillets
approx. 275ml/½ pint milk
2–3 tbsps sunflower oil
100g/4 oz button mushrooms, sliced
4 tomatoes, chopped
freshly ground black pepper
4 eggs
150ml/¼ pint soured cream

Put the fish in a pan and barely cover with milk. Bring to a slow boil, reduce the heat, cover and poach for 4–6 minutes until tender. Remove with a slotted spoon and place in an ovenproof dish. Cover and put in a moderate oven to keep warm. Bring the milk to a fast boil and reduce until only 3–4 tablespoons remain.

Meanwhile heat the oil in a frying pan, add the mushrooms and tomatoes and sauté for 5–6 minutes until they begin to soften. Season to taste with black pepper and spoon around the cooked fish. Poach the eggs and lay on top of the fish. Pour the soured cream into the pan containing the reduced milk and mix together well. Heat through, taking care not to boil. Pour over the poached eggs and serve immediately.

SARDINIAN BRILL

1–2 tbsps olive oil
350g/12 oz courgettes, sliced
450g/1 lb brill fillets
juice of 1 lemon
a good pinch of dried basil
25g/1 oz pine kernels
25g/1 oz sultanas
freshly ground black pepper

Heat the oil in a wok or large frying pan and stir-fry the courgettes for several minutes until they begin to soften. Cut the brill into thin strips about 2.5 cm/1 inch long, and toss into the pan. Cook for a minute or two before adding the remaining ingredients. Stir carefully to avoid breaking the strips of fish. Cook until the fish is tender. Serve immediately as a lunch or supper dish with fresh bread.

BUCKLING, *see* Smoked Fish

CLAMS

Clams have a fairly good culinary reputation, particularly in North America where clam chowder and clam bake can almost be described as national dishes. It is not easy to buy clams over here and I had to wait until my local Italian restaurant put *spaghetti alle vongole* on its menu for my first taste. Whether it was the fault of the chef or the clams remains to be seen, but the dish did not live up to expectations. The clams were nowhere near as tender or succulent as mussels and contained a disturbingly large amount of sand.

It is still worth looking out for fresh clams. They have the reputation of being 'hard nuts to crack', but there are several methods you can use to open the shells. You can try forcing them as if they were oysters, baking them in a hot oven like scallops, or steaming them as you would mussels. Once open, the clams can be grilled, fried or made into soups or sauces.

SPAGHETTI ALLE VONGOLE

12–15 small clams
150ml/¼ pint water
a sprig of fresh parsley
a sprig of fresh thyme
2–3 tbsps olive oil
2 cloves of garlic, peeled and crushed
1 tsp chopped anchovy fillets or anchovy paste
2 tbsps finely chopped fresh parsley
675g/1½ lbs ripe tomatoes, chopped
seasoning
450g/1 lb wholewheat spaghetti

Wash and scrub the clams thoroughly under cold running water, then put into a large pan with the water, parsley and thyme. Cover and cook over a high heat for 3–5 minutes, shaking the pan occasionally, until most have opened. Remove from the heat and when cool enough to handle remove and discard the opened shells. Chop the clams into two or three pieces unless they are already small, and keep aside until needed. Pass the liquid that remains in the bottom of the pan through a sieve lined with damp muslin, and reserve.

Heat the oil in a clean pan, add the garlic and sauté very gently for a minute or two, taking care not to brown. Add the anchovy fillets or paste, the chopped parsley, tomatoes and strained clam stock. Bring to the boil and simmer, uncovered, for 25–30 minutes, stirring occasionally, until the sauce thickens. Season to taste and stir in the chopped clams. Heat through.

Meanwhile cook the spaghetti until *al dente*. Drain and put into a large serving dish. Pour the sauce over the spaghetti and serve with crusty bread and a green salad.

COCKLES

Cockles are not in the same league as mussels but they can be used in pies, soups and salads. They can be rather tough and gritty and perhaps are best eaten when you are on holiday at the seaside with a portion of whelks and winkles.

COD

Cod was, until recently, the most important fish in our northern waters. Not only was it plentiful but it also had excellent keeping qualities and in bygone days inland communities relied upon supplies of salt and dried cod to see them through the numerous meatless days in the Christian calendar.

Dumas wrote in 1873 that, 'if no accident prevented the hatching of the eggs and if each egg reached maturity, it would take only three years to fill the sea so that you could walk across the Atlantic dry-shod on the backs of cod'. I am not sure whether the development of large deep-sea trawlers would class as an 'accident' but in the past forty years man has become the cod's most destructive predator and stocks have been devastated. Perhaps the great chef Escoffier is to be proved right, for he once remarked that if the cod was a much rarer fish we would all be after it.

Cod is a large, handsome fish, its bronzed skin dappled with greens and yellows. Inshore fish are reputed to have a better taste than those caught and frozen in Icelandic waters, but this is true only if they are really fresh. Good cod has big, firm, white, sweet tasting flakes which may have a curd between them rather like salmon. Too large to be displayed whole, cod is usually sold in steaks or fillets which can be poached, baked, fried, grilled, steamed and used in pies, croquettes and salads. Mushrooms, prawns, bacon, ham and most spices seem to have an affinity with the fish, and the addition of a sauce helps to keep the flakes moist and succulent. Unfortunately cod suffers badly from overcooking and loses both flavour and texture in the hands of a poor cook.

Available all year round, cod is at its best in the winter months. It is a fish which prefers icy waters, and when shoals of cod are spotted off our southern shores weather pundits immediately begin forecasting severe wintry conditions.

Salt cod is discussed separately under Salt Cod.

MALAYSIAN BAKED FISH

175ml/6 fl. oz water
50g/2 oz creamed coconut, chopped
a good pinch of saffron strands
½ tsp cardamom seeds
3 whole green cardamom pods
juice of ½ lemon
6 coriander seeds
1 carrot, chopped
1 bay leaf
4 cod steaks

Put all the ingredients, except for the fish, in a small pan and bring to the boil. Cover and simmer gently for 15 minutes. Pass through a sieve into a bowl. Dip the cod steaks into the sauce and then place in a shallow oven-proof dish. Pour over the remaining sauce and bake in a moderate oven, gas mark 5 (190° C/375° F) for 20–25 minutes until the fish is tender.

SCARBOROUGH PIE

A fish pie that originates from the fishing town of that name on the east coast of Yorkshire. It consists of an intriguing combination of the moist flakes of cod and the slightly chewier, saltier tang of fresh mussels.

150g/5 oz strong wholewheat bread flour
a good pinch of cream of tartar
90g/3½ oz butter   4–5 tbsps cold water
a little additional flour

FOR THE FILLING
450g/1 lb cod fillets, skinned
approx. 275ml/½ pint court-bouillon (p. 40)
100g/4 oz shelled mussels, chopped
grated rind of 1 large orange
a good pinch of ground mace
seasoning

FOR THE GLAZE
1 beaten egg

For the flaky pastry, mix the flour and cream of tartar together in a bowl. Add 25g/1 oz butter, chopped into a small pieces, and rub in with the fingertips. Pour the water over and mix into the flour with a fork to form a soft dough. Turn onto a floured board and knead for a minute or two until smooth. Wrap in polythene and put in a cool place for 30 minutes.

Sprinkle the remaining butter with flour and shape into a rectangle 1.25 cm/½ inch thick. Put the chilled dough on a lightly floured board and roll out to form a rectangle, slightly wider than the butter shape and long enough for the two ends to fold over the butter, overlapping slightly. Place the butter in the middle of the pastry dough and fold over the ends to cover it. Give the dough a half turn to bring the open ends to the top and bottom. Press the edges together to seal. Roll out the dough, quickly and lightly, to form an oblong 30 × 10 cm/12 × 4 inches. Mark the pastry into thirds, but don't cut through the dough, and then fold the bottom third over the middle and the top third down over both. Seal the edges and give the pastry a half turn. Repeat the rolling and folding once more, then wrap in polythene and chill for 30 minutes.

After two further rolls, folds and turns the pastry must rest again. Roll, fold and turn twice more. The pastry is now ready for use. Chill until needed.

For the filling, place the fish in a pan and barely cover with court-bouillon. Bring to a slow boil, cover, reduce the heat and poach for 4–6 minutes. Lift the fish from the pan with a slotted spoon, break into large flakes and place in a buttered ovenproof dish. Reserve the remaining court-bouillon (stock). Add the mussels, grated orange rind and mace. Season to taste. Bring the stock to the boil and boil briskly, uncovered, until reduced by half. Strain, leave to cool, then pour it – about 150ml/¼ pint – over the fish.

Roll out the pastry on a lightly floured board and cover the pie. Trim the pastry edges and brush the top with beaten egg – don't let the glaze run down the sides of the pastry or it won't rise evenly. Bake in a preheated oven, gas mark 8 (230° C/450° F), for 20–25 minutes.

SEAFOOD À LA FRANÇAISE

A rich, colourful fish stew made with cod fillets, mussels and prawns.

450g/1 lb mussels
150ml/¼ pint water
1–2 tbsps olive oil
2 onions, sliced
2 cloves of garlic, peeled and crushed
4 large tomatoes, chopped
150ml/¼ pint dry white wine
1 bay leaf
450g/1 lb cod fillets, skinned, boned and chopped
100g/4 oz peeled prawns
seasoning

Scrub the mussels under cold running water and pull away the beards. Discard any that are already open. Put them in a large pan with half the measured water. Cover and cook over a high heat for 3–4 minutes, tossing the pan occasionally, until most of the mussels have opened. Discard any that do not open. Remove the top shell from each mussel. Line a sieve with damp muslin and place over a bowl. Pass the cooking stock through the sieve. Keep both the stock and mussels on one side until needed.

Heat the oil in a casserole-type pan, add the onions and sauté until soft and golden. Add the garlic, tomatoes, the remaining water, the wine and bay leaf. Cover, bring to the boil and simmer for 15 minutes. Stir in the cod and poach for a further 4–5 minutes. Now add the mussels, their cooking stock and the prawns. Cook for 2–3 minutes more. Remove the bay leaf and season to taste.

COD IN A RICH TOMATO SAUCE

450g/1 lb tomatoes, chopped
1 clove of garlic, peeled and crushed
½ tsp dried oregano
½ tsp dried basil
2 tbsps lemon juice
3 tbsps water
1–2 tsps tomato purée (optional)
seasoning
675g/1½ lbs cod fillets, chopped into large pieces

Put the tomatoes, garlic, oregano, basil, lemon juice and water in a small pan. Bring to the boil, cover and simmer gently for 8–10 minutes, stirring occasionally, until the tomatoes have softened. Spoon the mixture into a food processor or blender and process until smooth or pass through a vegetable mouli. Depending on the quality and ripeness of the tomatoes it may be necessary to bolster up their flavour with a teaspoon or two of tomato purée. Season to taste.

Pour half the sauce into an ovenproof dish and arrange the fish on top. Cover with the remaining sauce and a tight fitting lid. Bake in a preheated oven, gas mark 5 (190° C/375° F), for 20–25 minutes.

Cod's roe

Looking rather like a pair of large, pink, elongated haggises, cod's roe can be seen at the fishmonger's in February. Both the soft male roe and the hard, granular female roe are usually sold ready boiled. All one needs to do is to slice and reheat them. In Cornwall and Ireland they were traditionally fried up with bacon and eaten for breakfast, but elsewhere it was customary to serve them with parsley sauce at teatime.

Smoked cod's roe is regarded as something of a delicacy and is eaten as an hors d'oeuvre with brown bread and lemon slices. It can also be used to make a sort of fish pâté, sometimes referred to as taramasalata, although I should point out that genuine taramasalata is made with the much scarcer roe of the grey mullet. See page 77 for recipe.

COLEY (coalfish, saithe, sillock)

Is it the relative cheapness of coley or its grey dingy appearance which has led many people to assume that it is only fit for their cats? Certainly it doesn't have the firmness or succulence of its close relative the cod, but it is still well worth buying. Its low cost makes it an ideal fish for use in pies, croquettes, soups and curries. You will find that the flesh whitens during cooking, especially if rubbed with lemon juice beforehand.

Coley is available throughout the year and is sold in steaks and fillets.

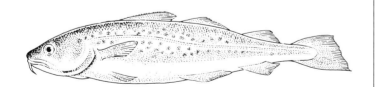

FISHCAKES

Use any white fish – coley, cod, haddock, whiting, etc.

Makes 8

450g/1 lb white fish fillets
approx. 275ml/½ pint milk
350g/12 oz potatoes, peeled and chopped
grated rind of 1 lemon
2 tsps Dijon mustard
3 tbsps finely chopped fresh parsley
seasoning

FOR THE COATING
1 large egg, beaten
100g/4 oz soft wholewheat breadcrumbs

Skin the fish and remove any bones. Put into a pan and barely cover with milk. Bring to a slow boil, reduce the heat, cover and poach for 4–6 minutes. Drain and reserve the milk. Meanwhile boil the potatoes until they too are tender. Drain and mash well with a little of the milk.

Put the cooked fish into a bowl and break into flakes. Add the potatoes, the grated lemon rind, mustard and parsley and mix together well. Season to taste. Add a little more milk if the mixture is too dry. Divide the mixture into eight pieces and press into shape. Dip the fishcakes first in the beaten egg and then in the breadcrumbs. Place them on an oiled baking tray and bake in a preheated oven, gas mark 6 (200° C/400° F), for 25–30 minutes. The fishcakes can be fried if you wish.

FISH CURRY WITH VEGETABLES

If you like curry spices but aren't too fond of the hot ones, take care when using chillies. Some are stronger than others, although there seems to be no way of knowing in advance which are hot and which are exceedingly hot. As a safeguard always remove and discard the white seeds from the centre of the chilli. This simple step will dramatically reduce the effectiveness of the chilli without losing any of its flavour. Chillies contain irritants which can actually 'burn' and raise blisters on the skin. Wash your hands as soon as you have finished chopping chillies, and refrain from touching your eyes or mouth.

½ **carrot, sliced**
2 **onions, sliced**
5 **black peppercorns**
1 **sprig of fresh parsley**
approx. 425ml/¾ **pint water**
450–675g/1–1½ **lbs coley fillets**
2–3 **tbsps groundnut oil**
2.5 cm/1 inch **fresh root ginger, peeled and grated**
2 **cloves of garlic, peeled and crushed**
2 **tbsps ground coriander**
1 **tsp black mustard seeds**
½ **tsp chilli powder**
a pinch of **asafoetida (optional)**
1 **potato, scrubbed and diced**
2 **green chillies, finely chopped**
4 **ripe tomatoes, diced**
225g/8 oz **mushrooms, chopped**
100g/4 oz **frozen peas**
2 **tsps garam masala**

Put the carrot, 1 slice of onion, peppercorns, parsley, water and coley in a pan. Bring to the boil, reduce the heat, cover and poach for 4–6 minutes until the fish is tender. Drain and reserve the stock. When cool enough to handle, skin the fish and remove any bones. Break into large flakes and keep aside until needed.

Heat the oil in a large heavy bottomed pan, add the remaining onion and sauté for 5–7 minutes until soft and golden. Add the ginger, garlic and spices and stir-fry for 2–3 minutes. Next add the potato, chillies, tomatoes, mushrooms and peas and stir well. Pour over 275ml/½ pint of the fish stock, cover and bring to the boil. Simmer gently for 8–10 minutes until the potatoes are tender. Stir the flaked fish carefully into the curried vegetables along with the garam masala. Heat through and serve with brown rice or chapati.

CONGER EEL

I remember all too well my first encounter with conger eel. The fishmonger pointed to a large box, inside which were entwined a mass of dark grey eels, with bodies as thick as my wrist. Hurriedly I averted my gaze, only to find myself staring into the eyes of four rather fierce looking eels stretched out on the marble stab. Finally, and to my immense relief, the fishmonger pointed to a row of neat, trim steaks whose white flesh glistened attractively against the dark grey skin.

Having made my purchase I went home and sat down with a couple of recipe books ready to be spurred into action by one or two delicious-sounding recipes. To my surprise, very few books mentioned conger eel at all, and those that did described it as 'having an insistent, almost unpleasant flavour' and 'a gelatinous, tough and close textured flesh'. As I was beginning to wonder what the rest of the family would make of conger eel and how best to disguise its insistent flavour and gelatinous flesh, I opened George Lassalles' *The Adventurous Fish Book* (Papermac, 1982) – a book which quite lives up to its name – and read, with much relief, that conger eel steaks are exceedingly good cooked with a rich tomato sauce. I tried it out for myself and must admit that it was just as good as Mr Lassalles promised.

Conger eel is all that its critics claim; it is fairly strongly flavoured, gelatinous and firm textured but, used in the right dishes, these qualities become positively advantageous. Conger eel is particularly good in soups and stews; it can also be poached or braised, and even roasted like meat. Off the coast of Brittany on Belle-Île it is known as *boeuf-bellilois*. Conger eel is fairly well respected on the Continent but this is not the case here in Britain. Most of our recipes originate from Cornwall where conger was popular with the miners, and there are many similarities between the old Cornish dishes and those found across the Channel in Normandy. What the British don't share is the French (and the Italian) passion for fish soup; conger eel is an important ingredient in *bouillabaisse, cotriade* and the Genovese *burrida*.

The first thing to understand about conger eel is that it is totally unrelated to the silvery freshwater eel which comes to our waters from the Sargasso Sea, and recipes for the two fish cannot be interchanged. Secondly, the number of bones increases alarmingly towards the tail, and unless making a stock or soup always choose thick middle cuts.

CURRIED CONGER EEL WITH YOGHURT

675g/1½ lbs conger eel steaks
1–2 tbsps sunflower oil
1 onion, finely chopped
2.5 cm/1 inch fresh root ginger, peeled and grated
1 clove of garlic, peeled and crushed
1 tbsp ground coriander
1 tsp black mustard seeds
1 tsp turmeric
1 green chilli, finely chopped
4 tomatoes, chopped
275ml/½ pint natural yoghurt
a good pinch of ground mace
50g/2 oz raisins
1–2 tbsps finely chopped fresh coriander

Put the conger eel steaks into a pan and barely cover with water (about 425ml/¾ pint). Bring to a slow boil, reduce the heat, cover and poach for 6–10 minutes. Drain the fish and discard the water. When cool enough to handle remove the skin and bones and chop into bite-sized pieces.

Heat the oil in a large heavy pan, add the onion and sauté for 5–7 minutes until soft and golden. Add the ginger, garlic and spices and stir-fry for a further 1–2 minutes. Now add the green chilli, tomatoes and yoghurt, bring to the boil and simmer, uncovered, for 20 minutes, stirring frequently until the sauce is greatly reduced and has thickened. Stir in the mace, raisins and cooked fish. Heat through and sprinkle with fresh coriander. Serve with brown rice or chapati.

BRAISED CONGER EEL WITH MUSHROOMS AND HERBS

4 conger eel steaks
2–3 tbsps olive oil
2 cloves of garlic, peeled and crushed
100g/4 oz button mushrooms, thinly sliced
juice of 2 lemons
1 tbsp finely chopped fresh parsley
1 tbsp finely chopped fresh thyme
seasoning
2 tomatoes, sliced

Remove the skin from each steak. To do this put the fish, skin uppermost, under a hot grill and cook until the surface begins to blister and brown. It will be necessary to turn each steak every now and then to expose all sides to the heat. Once the skin has been loosened in this way it is fairly easy to peel and scrape it away from the firm white meat.

Heat the oil in a frying pan, add the garlic and mushrooms and sauté for 2–3 minutes. Remove with a slotted spoon and place in the bottom of an ovenproof dish. Put the fish steaks into the pan and fry gently for 5 minutes on both sides. Then arrange them on top of the mushroom mixture. Pour over the lemon juice and sprinkle with the herbs and seasoning. Lay the tomatoes on the top and cover. Bake in a preheated oven, gas mark 5 (190° C/375° F), for 15–20 minutes until tender.

ROSY FISH PIES

4 conger eel steaks
approx. 425ml/¾ pint court-bouillon (p. 40)
1–2 tbsps olive oil
1 large Florence fennel bulb, chopped
2 cloves of garlic, peeled and crushed
4 tomatoes, chopped
seasoning

FOR THE SAUCE
20g/¾ oz butter
20g/¾ oz wholewheat flour

FOR THE PASTRY
225g/8oz wholewheat flour
75g/3 oz butter, diced
2 tbsps sunflower oil
8 tsps cold water
milk to glaze

Put the conger eel in a pan, pour over the court-bouillon and bring to a slow boil. Reduce the heat, cover and poach for 6–10 minutes until tender. Lift the fish from the pan with a slotted spoon and when cool enough to handle remove the skin and the bones. Cut the fish into bite-sized pieces and keep aside until needed. Also reserve the stock.

Heat the oil in a frying pan, add the fennel and garlic and sauté for 4–5 minutes. Add the tomatoes and cook for a further 3–4 minutes until they also begin to soften. Stir in the fish and season to taste. Remove from the heat.

To make the sauce, melt the butter in a pan and stir in the flour. Let the mixture bubble for several minutes before removing from the heat. Gradually add 350ml/ 12 fl. oz of the stock, stirring well after each addition. Return to the heat and bring to the boil, stirring continuously, until the sauce thickens. Pour over the fish and vegetable mixture and mix together well. Spoon into four individual pie dishes and leave to cool.

For the pastry, put the flour into a bowl, add the butter and oil and rub in, with the fingertips, until the mixture resembles breadcrumbs. Add the water and mix to form a dough. Turn onto a floured board and roll out. Cover the four pie dishes, trim the edges and brush with milk. Bake in a preheated oven, gas mark 6 (200° C/400° F), for 25 minutes.

CRABS

All crabs are edible but whether the effort of extracting the meat from some of the smaller ones is worthwhile is another matter. Here in Britain we tend to stick to just one variety, the red-backed crab, also known as the common crab.

Choose a crab which feels heavy for its size. If it has been boiled, look at the joint located at the back of the creature, between the upper and lower shells. While it is being cooked the shell of a well-filled crab should burst open a little. If this hasn't happened ask to look inside the shell before making your purchase. Most crabs are sold precooked today but sometimes, particularly if you buy direct from a fisherman, you may have to cook them at home. (Do make sure, however, that he kills it for you beforehand.) Once home, plunge the crab into a pan of boiling salted water and cook it for 25–35 minutes depending on size – 25 minutes will be sufficient for a specimen weighing 1–1.2kg/2–2½ lbs and 35 minutes for one 2kg/4½ lbs. A crab weighing 1–1.2kg/2–2½ lbs will be sufficient for two to three people.

Dressing a crab is easy provided that you are well endowed with patience. I used to enjoy helping my mother; we used the silver nutcracker set, breaking open the claws with the crackers and scraping out the white meat with the other implements. See pages 28–29 for directions as to how to remove the meat prior to dressing. Wash the empty top shell thoroughly and pat dry. The brown meat is rich and filling and some people find it difficult to digest, preferring to mix it with the white meat or some soft breadcrumbs. Spoon the seasoned brown meat into the shell and arrange the white meat on top. Garnish before serving. Dressed crabs look attractive and taste delicious – some say they are even better than lobster and they are certainly much cheaper.

Many fishmongers sell packets of frozen crab meat which, although not as finely flavoured as fresh meat, are useful in other ways: crab soup and soufflés, flans and tarts, pâtés and spreads are all well worth making.

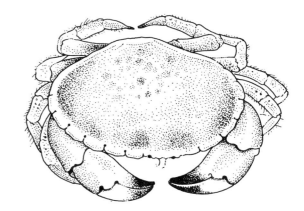

CRAB BISQUE

Serves 4–6
2 medium-sized boiled crabs
25g/1 oz butter
½ onion, sliced
1 carrot, sliced
1 sprig of fresh parsley
2 tbsps brandy
1.2 litres/2 pints fumet/fish stock (p. 41)
150ml/¼ pint dry white wine
50g/2 oz long grain brown rice
seasoning

Break open the crab shells and extract both the brown and white meat, placing them in separate bowls. Discard the claws and spongy gills but retain the rest of the shells and the legs. Melt the butter in a large pan, add the onion, carrot and parsley and sauté for 5–7 minutes. Warm the brandy and pour it, flaming, into the pan. Add 850ml/1½ pints of the fumet, the wine and broken shells. Bring to the boil, cover and simmer for 20 minutes. Strain the stock into a bowl and pound the vegetables and the shells with a pestle (or the end of a rolling pin) for 4–5 minutes. Return the stock to the pounded ingredients and stir well. Strain again, this time discarding the solids.

In the meantime, cook the rice in the remaining 275ml/½ pint fumet until soft. Place the brown crab meat, the cooked rice and the strained stock in a food processor or liquidiser and process until smooth. Pass through a sieve and pour into a clean pan. Stir in the flakes of white crab meat and heat through. Season to taste before serving.

CRAB SOUFFLÉ

For some reason a certain amount of glamour and awe is attached to the soufflé, so much so that many people view making one with a great deal of trepidation. Stories abound about collapsed and runny soufflés, and it is hardly surprising that we become uneasy. My mother has the right idea: she pooh-poohs such stories and says that there is nothing difficult about making a soufflé. After all, it is only a richly flavoured thick white sauce, into which are folded stiffly beaten egg whites. The whole mixture is then baked until well risen and firm – what could be simpler?

250ml/9 fl. oz milk
1 slice of onion
1 bay leaf
6 black peppercorns
40g/1½ oz butter
1 shallot, finely chopped
15g/½ oz unbleached white flour
2 tbsps natural yoghurt
4 egg yolks
225g/8 oz brown crab meat
a good pinch of cayenne pepper
freshly grated nutmeg
6 egg whites

Put the milk, onion, bay leaf and black peppercorns in a pan and bring to the boil. Remove from the heat and leave to infuse for 15–20 minutes. Strain.

Melt the butter in another pan, add the shallot and sauté for 3–4 minutes until soft and golden. Stir in the flour and cook for a minute or two more until the mixture begins to bubble. Remove from the heat and gradually add the strained milk, stirring well after each addition. Return to the heat and bring to the boil, stirring frequently, until the sauce thickens. Once again remove from the heat. Beat the yoghurt and egg yolks together before stirring into the sauce. Add the crab meat and season well with cayenne pepper and nutmeg.

Whisk the egg whites until stiff and peaked, and fold into the mixture. Spoon into a buttered soufflé dish and bake in a preheated oven, gas mark 7 (220° C/425° F), for 10–15 minutes. Serve immediately.

CUTTLEFISH

Cuttlefish are perhaps the most unattractive of all the cephalopods but don't let looks put you off. They are considered much finer to eat than either the squid or octopus. They have the same delicious, sweet tasting meat but are much more tender. Many of the best recipe ideas have originated from the Mediterranean, for it is here that their culinary charms are truly appreciated. Tomatoes, olive oil, wine and garlic feature in many cuttlefish dishes and I particularly like *seppie con spinaci* from Tuscany. If the idea of cooking cuttlefish with spinach seems a little strange, don't worry – it is a marriage that must have been made in heaven for the two complement each other perfectly.

SEPPIE CON SPINACI

1 kg/2–2¼ lbs cuttlefish
1–2 tbsps olive oil
2 onions, chopped
2–3 cloves of garlic, peeled and crushed
2–3 tbsps chopped green celery leaves
150ml/¼ pint red wine
150ml/¼ pint water
1–2 tbsps tomato purée
seasoning
100g/4 oz frozen chopped spinach

Prepare the cuttlefish as described on page 25–26. Look out for the thin, silvery ink sacs and keep one back. Chop the cleaned cuttlefish into bite-sized pieces.

Heat the oil in a heavy pan, add the onions, garlic and celery leaves and sauté for 5–7 minutes until soft and golden. Add the cuttlefish and sauté for 3–4 minutes more. Pour the wine and water into the pan and stir in the contents of the ink sac and the tomato purée. Bring to the boil, cover and simmer for 30–40 minutes. Add the spinach and cook for a further 5–10 minutes until the cuttlefish is tender. Season to taste.

DABS

Dabs are small flat fish which have tended to be over-shadowed by the slightly larger plaice. They taste as good and can be cooked in similar ways. They are especially good grilled or fried, either filleted or whole, and served with a light sauce. Remove the dark skin when cooking dabs whole, but don't bother when serving fillets – they are thin enough as it is. Like plaice, dabs have a soft texture and should not be overcooked. Fillets cook under a hot grill in 3–5 minutes. Never throw away the heads and bones without first making some fish stock. Good stock is worth its weight in gold, particularly now that so many of our fish come ready-filleted. Dabs are best in the late autumn and early winter.

GRILLED DABS WITH PARSLEY SAUCE

4 dabs
½ carrot, sliced
2 slices of onion
4 black peppercorns
1 small bay leaf
sunflower oil

FOR THE SAUCE
15g/½ oz butter
1 tbsp sunflower oil
25g/1 oz unbleached white flour
275ml/½ pint milk
1 tbsp finely chopped fresh parsley
1 tsp Dijon mustard
seasoning

Clean and fillet the dabs. Discard the viscera. Keep to one side until needed. Put what is left of the fish, heads included, into a saucepan with the carrot, onion, black peppercorns and bay leaf and barely cover with water. Bring to the boil, cover and simmer gently for 15–20 minutes. Strain well and return the stock to the pan. Bring to the boil again and boil briskly, uncovered, until reduced by half.

For the sauce, melt the butter and oil in a pan and stir in the flour. Cook for a minute or two, letting the mixture bubble, and stirring often to prevent it sticking. Remove from the heat and gradually add the milk and 150ml/ ¼ pint reduced stock, stirring well after each addition. Return to the heat and bring to the boil, stirring all the time, until the sauce begins to thicken. Add the parsley and mustard and season to taste. Keep warm.

Place the fish fillets skin side downwards on an oiled baking tray. Brush with oil and put under a hot grill. Cook for 3–5 minutes. Serve immediately with the sauce.

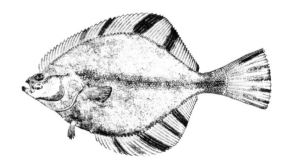

DOGFISH

Dog fish, cat fish, wolf fish, Scarboro' woof, rock salmon, rock turbot, huss, flake and rigg are some of the names given to the varieties of small sharks caught off our coasts. Shunned by the general public they are eaten, heavily disguised in batter, by thousands of unsuspecting customers at fish and chip shops up and down the country.

Available for most of the year, they are all well worth buying and are especially good in pies, stews and curries. The flesh is firm and well flavoured; my fishmonger calls them poor man's halibut, while others claim that they taste like veal.

FILEY'S GOOD FRIDAY PIE

A real Good Friday treat. My fishmonger says that up until a couple of years ago he sold four times as much fish on Good Friday than on any other day of the year. Customs and traditions do die but let's hope that the old recipes themselves will live on.

500g/1–1¼ lbs Scarboro' woof fillets
1 bay leaf
450ml/16 fl. oz milk
4 rashers of bacon, trimmed and chopped
seasoning
3 hard-boiled eggs, sliced
225g/8 oz potatoes, cooked and sliced
50g/2 oz butter
50g/2 oz unbleached white flour
450g/1 lb wholewheat puff pastry
a little beaten egg or milk

Put the fish in a pan with the bay leaf and pour the milk over. Bring to a slow boil, reduce the heat, cover and poach for 4–6 minutes. Drain and reserve the milk. Discard the bay leaf. Cut the fish into bite-sized pieces and place in a pie dish. Fry the bacon and when cooked scatter over the fish. Season to taste. Place the slices of hard-boiled egg and cooked potato on top.

Melt the butter in a saucepan and stir in the flour and cook gently until the mixture begins to bubble. Remove from the heat and gradually add the reserved milk, stirring well after each addition. Return to the heat and bring to the boil, stirring continuously until the sauce thickens. Lightly mix with the fish mixture and leave to cool.

Divide the pastry into four pieces and roll out to form identical squares, measuring approximately 20 ×20 cm/8 ×8 inches. Spread the filling over the top, leaving a good margin clear around the edge. Brush the pastry edges with water and form an envelope by bringing the four corners up to the centre. Press the sides together to seal. Decorate with pastry shapes, made from the trimmings, and brush with a little milk or beaten egg to glaze.

Carefully lift on to a lightly oiled baking tray and bake in a preheated oven, gas mark 7 (220° C/425° F), for 30 minutes.

You could, of course, make one large family-sized pie.

PANCAKES WITH DOGFISH AND CIDER STUFFING

Although pancakes can be made and cooked fairly quickly, it is sometimes useful, particularly when cooking for a large number, to prepare them in advance. Interleaved with greaseproof paper and sealed inside a polythene bag they will keep in the refrigerator for several days, or for 2–3 months in a deep freeze.

Makes 12
225g/8 oz wholewheat flour
a pinch of salt (optional)
4 eggs, beaten
350ml/12 fl. oz milk

FOR THE FILLING
2 leeks, thinly sliced
175ml/6 fl. oz milk
350g/12 oz dogfish fillets, chopped
40g/1½ oz butter
40g/1½ oz wholewheat flour
175ml/6 fl. oz dry cider
2 tbsps finely chopped fresh parsley
seasoning

To make the batter, put the flour and salt (if using it) in a bowl and make a well in the centre. Pour the beaten eggs and half the milk into the well and stir in the flour, a little at a time. Mix to form a smooth batter. Gradually add the rest of the milk and beat well until frothy. The batter can easily be made in a blender or food processor; put all the ingredients in the goblet and process until smooth and creamy. Cook the pancakes in the usual way and stack until needed.

For the filling steam the leeks until barely tender. Put the milk in a pan and add the fish. Bring to a slow boil, reduce the heat, cover and poach for 4–6 minutes. When cooked, drain and reserve both the fish and the milk.

Melt the butter in a clean pan and stir in the flour. Let the mixture bubble for a minute or two, stirring frequently, before removing from the heat. Gradually add the reserved milk and the cider, stirring well after each addition. Return to the heat and bring to the boil, stirring all the time, until the sauce thickens. Add the cooked leeks, fish and the parsley. Season to taste.

Spoon two tablespoons of the filling onto each pancake, roll up like a Swiss roll and arrange in the bottom of a shallow ovenproof dish. Repeat until all the filling and all the pancakes have been used up. Put into a preheated oven, gas mark 6 (200° C/400° F), for 15–20 minutes until heated through.

DOVER SOLE

Dover sole is generally recognised as being the best fish to come out of our cold northern waters. Not only has it a delicate flavour but also a firm, succulent texture which even the most slap-happy cook would find difficult to overcook. Chefs and restaurateurs love it because it is said to improve if kept for a day or two, and it is one of the few white fish which can be left to wait in the serving dish without coming to too much harm.

As a rule sole are only filleted when they are to be served with a sauce. If you order filleted fish from the fishmonger remember to take the heads and bones away with you as they make excellent stock. The skin of the sole is unusually thick and the dark skin is always removed. It is a matter of taste whether you remove the white skin or not.

You will need about 175–225g/6–8 oz per person.

Large thick fish can be disappointing in flavour, and all sole are good treated plainly. Grilled and served with melted butter, parsley and lemon is one of the finest ways of preparing them, although sole in general lend themselves to almost any cooking method.

SOLE À LA MEUNIÈRE

This dish, one of the mainstays of fish cooking, was first credited (or so the name implies) not to one of the great French chefs but to a miller's wife. Whether by instinct or training, she was an excellent cook and fully appreciated that fresh fish is best served plain with little in the way of accompaniments or garnishes. What could be nicer than a really fresh trout or sole lightly browned in butter? Fish cooked *à la meunière* is difficult to prepare for more than two people as it must be rushed to the table while the butter is sizzlingly hot.

100g/4 oz butter
4 Dover sole fillets
wholewheat flour for dusting

Clarify the butter (see p. 49) and then heat in a large frying pan until frothy. Dust the fillets in flour and then slip them into the hot butter. Cook for 2–4 minutes on each side until golden brown and rush to the table while the butter is still foaming. If the butter has become blackened during cooking carefully lift the fillets from the pan and drain on absorbent paper. Clean out the pan and add 50g/2 oz butter. Heat until it melts and begins to froth and brown. Arrange the fish on a serving dish, pour over the hot butter and take to the table.

SOLE WITH WINE SAUCE AND ALMONDS

The topping used in this recipe is a little out of the ordinary. The sauce is delicately flavoured with wine and is covered with a layer of ground almonds followed by some crunchy flaked almonds.

4 Dover sole fillets
a knob of butter

FOR THE SAUCE
25g/1 oz butter
25g/1 oz unbleached white flour
100ml/4 fl. oz dry white wine
175ml/6 fl. oz milk
seasoning
15g/½ oz ground almonds
15g/½ oz flaked almonds

Put the fish in a buttered ovenproof dish, dab the knob of butter over the top, and cover with greaseproof paper. Bake in a preheated oven, gas mark 5 (190° C/375° F), for 15 minutes until tender.

Meanwhile make the sauce. Melt the 25g/1 oz butter in a small pan and stir in the flour. Cook until the mixture begins to bubble. Remove from the heat and gradually add the wine and milk, stirring well after each addition. Return to the heat and bring to the boil, stirring all the time, until the sauce thickens. Season to taste, and pour over the cooked fillets. Sprinkle the ground almonds and then the flaked almonds over the top. Put under a hot grill or in a hot oven until the nuts begin to brown and the sauce is hot and bubbling.

DOVER SOLE WITH CUCUMBER AND MUSHROOMS

An unusual but excellent way of serving Dover sole. It is taken to the table in its own light buttery sauce and is delicious served with new potatoes.

25–50g/1–2 oz butter
¼ cucumber, diced
100g/4 oz button mushrooms, sliced
2 Dover sole, filleted
freshly ground black pepper
juice of ½ lemon

Melt the butter in a pan, add the cucumber and mushrooms and sauté for 4–5 minutes. Cut the fillets into bite-sized pieces and toss into the pan. Cover and cook for a further 3–4 minutes, stirring occasionally, until the fish is tender. Season to taste with black pepper and lemon juice. Serve.

DUBLIN BAY PRAWNS

Whether you see them labelled as Dublin Bay prawns, Norway prawns, scampi or langoustines, there is no mistaking this pink shellfish. It resembles a lobster, complete with claws, but is no more than 25 cm/ 10 inches long. Like the lobster the edible meat is to be found in the abdomen and tail. For four people you will need to buy 900g/2 lbs, or half that amount if they are already shelled.

It is a pity that fresh Dublin Bay prawns are so rarely available in our shops for they are delicious. If you are lucky enough to find some, poach them in lightly salted water for no more than 10 minutes and serve them hot in their shells with a hollandaise sauce or melted butter, or cold with *aïoli* or mayonnaise. Part of the fun is to shell them, one by one, at the table, dipping the edible tail into the sauce before popping it into one's mouth.

Frozen 'scampi' tails are more readily available and, although not in the same league as fresh ones, are still worth buying. They are popular coated in batter and deep-fried, but are even nicer marinated in oil and lemon juice and then grilled or cooked over a barbecue.

FRITTO MISTO DI MARE

This dish is popular in Italy, and as the name suggests it consists of deep-fried seafoods. Sometimes only two or three types are used but on other occasions as many as half a dozen may be included. The selection of fish depends very much on what is available on the day you are planning to make the dish.

Prawns, small red mullet and squid are a popular combination in Italy, but I like to add a few whitebait and some firm white fish chopped into bite-sized pieces.

Serves 4–6
**1kg–2–2¼ lbs assorted fish
(Dublin Bay prawns, peeled prawns, baby squid, whitebait, monkfish, halibut, dogfish)**

FOR THE BATTER
**50g/2 oz wholewheat flour
50g/2 oz unbleached white flour
a pinch of salt (optional)
150ml/¼ pint water
2 tbsps sunflower oil
1 egg white**

Poach, shell and de-vein the Dublin Bay prawns if using them. Prepare the squid as described on page 25 and then slice the sac-like bodies into 1.25-cm/½-inch rings. Put the squid into a pan of simmering water and cover. Poach gently until tender; depending on the size and age of the squid this can take anything from 5–20 minutes. When tender drain well and pat dry with a cloth. The whitebait can be cooked just as they are, but the white fish needs to be chopped into bite-sized pieces and any skin and bones discarded. It is best to keep each variety of fish in a separate container.

To make the batter, mix the two flours together in a bowl and add the salt if using it. Make a well in the centre and pour in the water. Gradually work into the flours, mixing well until smooth. Add the oil and beat vigorously until the surface is covered in bubbles. Whisk the egg white until peaked, and fold into the mixture. If using a blender or food processor put the flours, salt, water and oil into the goblet and process until smooth. Spoon into a bowl. Whisk the egg white until stiff and peaked and then fold into the mixture.

Meanwhile, half-fill a deep pan with oil and heat to 190° C/375° F. Test with a cook's thermometer or by dropping a small cube of bread into the hot fat; it should brown in about half a minute if the fat is hot enough. Dip the fish into the batter and then place them in the hot fat, a few at a time. Fry for 2–3 minutes until golden brown. Drain on absorbent paper and keep warm until all the fish is cooked. Serve as soon as possible.

Don't be too ambitious when planning a *fritto misto* dish. It is much better to make it in small quantities and to serve it as a starter, otherwise you may find yourself tied to a hot stove, for as fast as you turn out the dainty golden fritters your family or friends will be back for more.

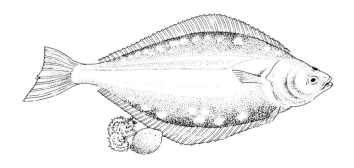

FRESHWATER EELS

I saw my first freshwater eels while on holiday at Pont Aberglaslyn in Wales when I was very young. The tiny dark grey elvers, between 2.5–5 cm/1–2 inches long, were wriggling and squirming their way up the mountain river, resting every so often in a shallow pool before tackling the next waterfall. My father told me how they had just swum thousands of miles from the Sargasso Sea in the Atlantic and were now on the last leg of their journey. I remember wishing that we could help them, for they looked so small and helpless against the black rocks and rushing water. Having reached their destination the elvers would spend several years maturing before making the return journey. Those that escaped the fishermen's nets would swim back to the Sargasso Sea to spawn and eventually die.

Not so long ago freshwater eels were fairly commonplace and were regarded as something of a delicacy by rich and poor alike. Old cookery books are full of recipes for jellied eels, stewed eels, eels and mash, elvers in the Gloucester or Tewkesbury way, and, perhaps most famous of all, London's eel pie. Eel pie was the speciality of a pub on Eel Pie Island, Richmond. People flocked there to enjoy a day's boating, fishing, picnicking and, of course, to sample the pie. The island is still there, just across the river from Twickenham, but unfortunately the pub and its grub have long since gone and now large notices posted on the bridge make it clear that day trippers are no longer welcome.

Although few of us are ever likely to have the opportunity to eat eel pie, a plate of jellied eels is quite another matter. They can still be bought at many seaside resorts, especially those in the West Country, and in the East End of London. The eels are cleaned and chopped into pieces before being simmered gently in court-bouillon. As they cool the stock thickens to a stiff jelly, which is served with the cooked fish. Traditionally jellied eels were eaten with boiled potatoes and horseradish sauce, but nowadays it is more usual to eat them sprinkled with vinegar while walking along the seafront or promenade.

Unfortunately freshwater eels are seldom seen in our shops today. When they are available they are usually sold live, and it is worth remembering that eels carry on wriggling for several hours after they have been killed. It is also said that the eel's blood is poisonous if it comes in contact with a flesh wound, at any rate until the fish is cooked. All in all it seems wise, if you are not familiar with these slippery creatures, to ask the fisherman or fishmonger to kill, skin and chop them for you.

Smoked eels are now regarded by many as a great delicacy, eaten plainly with slices of buttered brown bread.

MATELOTE D'ANGUILLES

I have taken this recipe from Jane Grigson's book *Fish Cookery* (Wine and Food Society, 1973).

Serves 6–8

1.3–1.8kg/3–4 lbs freshwater eel, skinned and cut up
3–4 tbsps marc or brandy
4 tbsps oil
1 bottle red wine
175g/6 oz onion or shallot, chopped
white of 1 leek, chopped (optional)
2 cloves of garlic, peeled and crushed (optional)
bouquet garni
1½ tbsps flour
25g/1 oz butter
seasoning

FOR THE GARNISH
20–30 small glazed onions
20–30 small button mushrooms, cooked in butter
triangles of bread fried in butter
chopped parsley

Turn the pieces of eel in the brandy and oil, season well and leave for several hours or overnight.

A good hour before the meal, simmer the wine with the onion, leek, garlic, and bouquet garni for half an hour. Arrange the eels in a large pan and strain the seasoned wine over them. The eel should just be covered. Stew gently for 20–30 minutes until the eel is cooked.

Mash the flour and butter together, dividing the mixture into small lumps, then add them gradually to the red wine stew, stirring all the time so that the sauce thickens smoothly. Correct the seasoning, pour into a serving dish and arrange the hot glazed onions and button mush-

rooms on the top. Dip one corner of each triangle of fried bread in the stew and then in the chopped parsley. Tuck into the stew, parsley uppermost.

FINNAN HADDOCK, *see* Smoked Fish

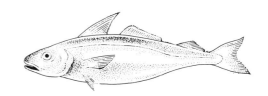

GARFISH

Garfish is becoming an increasingly common sight at the fishmonger's, arriving off our shores just ahead of the mackerel in February and March. It is easily recognised, being one of the most elegant and unusual-looking fish. At the end of its long slender body is a 5 cm/2 inch 'beak' complete with tiny teeth. The skin is a shimmering peacock blue, a colour which is seen again when the fish is cut open, for against the white flesh lies a network of electric-blue bones. Unfortunately, whereas I find them particularly attractive and try to make a feature of them, many more people are horrified by the discovery, worrying in case the fish isn't wholesome. They need not fear, for the garfish is a very tasty fish with a firm texture and good flavour. It is usual to cut garfish into steaks, but it can be filleted. In either case it is excellent poached, braised, grilled or fried.

CASSEROLED GARFISH

1–2 garfish, weighing 675–900g/1½–2 lbs in all
1–2 tbsps olive oil
2 sticks of celery, chopped
1 clove of garlic, peeled and crushed
1 onion, chopped
450g/1 lb tomatoes, chopped
100g/4 oz mushrooms, chopped
1 tbsp finely chopped fresh thyme
1 tbsp white wine vinegar
150ml/¼ pint water
seasoning

Clean the fish, remove and discard the fins, heads and tails. Wash carefully and pat dry. Cut into 2.5 cm/1 inch steaks.

Heat the oil in a heavy casserole-type pan, add the celery, garlic and onion and sauté for 5–7 minutes until soft and golden. Add the tomatoes, mushrooms and thyme and cook for a further 4–5 minutes. Arrange the fish in the bottom of the pan and pour over the vinegar and water. Bring to a very slow boil, reduce the heat, cover and poach for 5–8 minutes until the fish is tender. Season to taste.

GARFISH POACHED IN WINE

1–2 garfish, weighing 675–900g/1½–2 lbs in all
75g/3 oz butter
2 onions, chopped
2 leeks, chopped
275ml/½ pint dry white wine
275ml/½ pint court-bouillon (p. 40)
25g/1 oz unbleached white flour
seasoning
1 tbsp finely chopped fresh chives

Clean the fish, remove and discard the heads, tails and fins. Wash carefully and pat dry. Cut into 2.5-cm/1-inch pieces.

Melt 25g/1 oz of the butter in a pan, add the onions and leeks and sauté until soft and golden. Lay the fish on top of the vegetables and pour the wine and court-bouillon over it. Bring to a slow boil, reduce the heat, cover and poach for 5–8 minutes until the garfish is tender. Lift the fish and vegetables out of the pan with a slotted spoon and put into a shallow ovenproof serving dish. Pour over 2–3 tablespoons of the cooking stock. Cover and keep warm in a moderate oven.

Work the remaining butter and the flour together with the fingertips to form a *beurre manié*. Shape into small balls about the size of marbles. Bring the remaining cooking stock to a slow boil and drop in the butter balls, three or four at a time, stirring frequently until they have melted. Then add a few more butter balls and so on until all the balls have been incorporated into the stock. Continue to cook gently until the sauce begins to thicken. Season to taste and pour over the fish and vegetables. Sprinkle with the chives. Serve with brown rice or potatoes.

GREY MULLET

'It is a sore point with the red mullet that an inferior race with whom they have no relations whatever should swim the sea, and be known to fame as grey mullets. Grey they may be, but mullets they are not' (*Kettner's Book of the Table*, 1877).

It is generally recognised that grey mullets are not in the same culinary league as red mullets but that is not to say that they should be ignored. They are available throughout the year at a fairly modest price, and when cooked properly can be very good indeed. I grill or bake them as they seem to become unpleasantly soft if poached or braised.

The grey mullet is usually sold whole. It is slightly too plump to be described as svelte but is still fairly stream-lined. The scales on its grey back and striped silvery sides are large and thick and care must be taken when removing them for the skin underneath is delicate and easily torn. The fish is unusual in that it seems to be able to adjust to any degree of salinity and spends as much time grubbing about on the bottom of our estuaries and tidal rivers as it does in the open sea. This has resulted in a reputation for it tasting muddy, but I have never encountered this problem. I believe that most of the grey mullet on sale in the shops are caught in the open sea off the coasts of Cornwall and Devon so perhaps the problem is confined to fish caught by rod and line.

Large whole fish can be cooked *en papillote* and many books recommend gutting them through the gills and filling the cavity with a savoury stuffing. Smaller ones are good brushed with olive oil and grilled, ideally over charcoal, and served with a savoury butter. Fillets can be baked, grilled or fried and eaten with any number of sauces.

Grey mullet are much sought after in the Mediterranean where the roe is regarded as a great delicacy. It is used to make authentic taramasalata and a much firmer sausage-shaped pâté known as *botargo* which is served with thin slices of bread and either olive oil or butter.

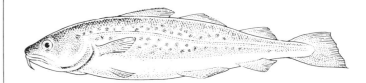

TARAMASALATA

As grey mullet roe is seldom available, cod's roe can be used in its place.

175g/6 oz grey mullet roe or smoked cod's roe
100g/4 oz low-fat cream cheese
1–2 tbsps olive oil
1 tbsp lemon juice

Mix all the ingredients together until smooth. Serve as a spread or dip with brown bread, toast or pitta.

GURNARD

Gurnards are colourful creatures, being either grey, yellow or red. Although the grey gurnard is the most common visitor to our waters, we are more likely to see the red one in the shops. At first glance it can easily be mistaken for a red mullet but on closer inspection it is found to be quite different. The gurnard is lean and bony with a row of sharp, spiky fins running along its back and belly. The head is abnormally large and the scales around its gills stand out like armour plating.

Many cooks choose to bake the gurnard whole, first removing the fins and then cleaning it through the gills. In view of my comments on its appearance this may seem rather perverse, but it is done more for economic reasons than on account of the gurnard's 'surrealistic charm'. The head is so large that if it were to be removed there would be very little left! Choose fish weighing at least 225g/8 oz per person. Fillets can be lifted from the bone and then poached, grilled, baked or fried.

The flesh is firm and white and on more than one occasion has been mistaken for chicken when cooked in a pie. Always use the head to make stock. Small gurnards are excellent additions to fish soups, especially *bouillabaisse*.

GURNARD AND FENNEL PIE

675g/1½ lbs red gurnard
425ml/¾ pint milk
½ carrot, sliced
1 slice of onion   1 bay leaf
2 sprigs of fresh parsley
1 sprig of fresh thyme
6 black peppercorns
1–2 tbsps olive oil
1 large Florence fennel bulb, sliced

FOR THE SAUCE
15g/½ oz butter
1 tbsp sunflower oil
25g/1 oz wholewheat flour
seasoning

FOR THE PASTRY
175g/6 oz wholewheat flour
75g/3 oz butter, diced
6 tsps cold water

Clean the fish, put into a pan and barely cover with milk. Add the carrot, onion, bay leaf, parsley, thyme and black peppercorns. Bring to a slow boil, reduce the heat, cover and poach for 5–8 minutes until tender. Lift the fish from the pan with a slotted spoon and when cool enough to handle remove the skin. Lift the flesh from the bones and break into large flakes. Keep aside until needed. Strain the milk and reserve that too.

Heat the olive oil in a pan, add the fennel and sauté for 5–7 minutes until it begins to soften. To make the sauce, heat the butter and sunflower oil in a pan and then stir in the flour. Let the mixture bubble for a minute or two before removing from the heat. Gradually stir in 350ml/12 fl. oz milk stock, stirring well after each addition. Return the pan to the stove and heat gently, stirrng frequently, until the sauce begins to thicken. Pour over the fennel. Stir in the cooked fish and season to taste. Spoon the mixture into a pie dish.

To make the pastry, put the flour in a bowl and rub in the butter, with the fingertips, until the mixture resembles breadcrumbs. Add the water and mix to form a dough. Roll out on a lightly floured board and cover the pie dish. Trim the edges and dampen with a little water. Press to seal. Brush with some of the remaining milk stock. Bake in a preheated oven, gas mark 6 (200° C/400° F), for 25 minutes.

MARINATED GURNARD, INDIAN STYLE

1 heaped tsp cardamom seeds, crushed
1 heaped tsp ground cumin
1 heaped tsp ground coriander
½ level tsp ground cloves
½ level tsp ground cinnamon
½ level tsp ground mace
150ml/¼ pint natural yoghurt
4 gurnard
1–2 tbsps groundnut oil

Mix the spices and yoghurt together in a bowl and set aside.

Clean the fish and remove the spiky fins. Wash and dry carefully before making four to five diagonal gashes on both sides of each fish. Extend the belly opening down to the tail. Then, with a small spoon or blunt knife, work the spicy yoghurt into the openings. Arrange the fish on a large baking tray or dish and spoon any remaining yoghurt mixture over the top. Leave to stand in a cool place for 6 hours or so. If the fish are very fresh they can be left overnight.

Carefully scrape any excess yoghurt from the gurnard before brushing them with oil. Lay each fish on its side on a baking tray lined with foil. Place under a hot grill and cook for 5–7 minutes on each side.

Serve with new potatoes and a salad.

H

HADDOCK

Not so long ago, when cod was cheap and plentiful, haddock was considered far superior and there was a certain amount of kudos attached to its name. The cod war put paid to all that and now the haddock has replaced the cod as the most important commercial catch, and its reputation is that of being a useful but uninspiring fish, ideal for everyday dishes. Haddock is available all the year round and is at its best in the winter and early spring. Sold in fillets it can be poached, baked, fried, grilled or used in pies and casseroles.

As time goes by I find myself buying less and less haddock, with one exception – smoked haddock. I don't mean those garish fillets sold locally as golden cutlets but the genuine oak-smoked product. The Scots are the undisputed masters of this craft and the magnificent Finnan haddock is one of their greatest achievements. See the section on Smoked Fish (page 134).

HADDOCK CHOWDER

1 onion, finely chopped
4 slices salt pork/streaky bacon, chopped
5 potatoes, peeled and diced
1 litre/1¾ pints milk
1kg/2–2¼ lbs haddock fillets, chopped
25g/1 oz butter, diced
freshly ground black pepper

Sauté the onion and salt pork together. Add the potatoes and milk. Bring to the boil, cover and simmer for 6–8 minutes. Add the fish and continue to cook until the fish and potatoes are tender. Stir in the butter and pepper.

HADDOCK FRICASSÉE

Lightly cooked fish bathed in a yoghurt sauce delicately flavoured with thyme and nutmeg.

675g/1½ lbs haddock fillets
100g/4 oz button mushrooms, halved if necessary
100g/4 oz frozen peas
425ml/¾ pint natural yoghurt
1 heaped tbsp unbleached white flour
2 eggs (optional)
2 tsps finely chopped fresh thyme
freshly grated nutmeg

Skin the fish and chop into bite-sized pieces. Put into a pan with the mushrooms and peas. Mix the yoghurt and flour together and beat in the eggs, if using them. (The eggs add colour and richness to the sauce.) Pour over the fish and season with thyme and nutmeg. Bring to the boil, reduce the heat, cover and cook gently for 4–6 minutes, stirring occasionally, until the sauce thickens and the fish becomes tender. Serve with wholewheat pasta.

SPICY FISH BALLS

Almost any white fish can be used to make these fish balls but don't waste your money on expensive varieties. Haddock, whiting or coley are a much better buy.

There are some dishes, such as *fritto misto*, which must be deep-fried and perhaps once a year I reluctantly bring out the chip pan rather than miss such a treat, but I don't like deep-frying foods and whenever possible I look for alternative cooking methods. These spicy fish balls, for example, can be baked successfully in a preheated oven, gas mark 6 (200° C/400° F), for 20–25 minutes until golden brown.

Serves 4–6
1–2 tbsps groundnut oil
1 onion, finely chopped
2 cloves of garlic, peeled and crushed
2 green chillies, finely chopped
1 tsp turmeric
1 tsp ground coriander
1 tsp ground cumin
450g/1 lb white fish fillets, cooked
2 tbsps finely chopped fresh coriander
2 tsps lemon juice
450g/1 lb potatoes, cooked and mashed
seasoning
2 eggs, beaten
100g/4 oz soft wholewheat breadcrumbs
oil for deep-frying

Heat the groundnut oil in a large frying pan, add the onion and garlic and sauté for 5–7 minutes until soft and golden. Stir in the green chillies and the spices and stir-fry for a minute or two more. Lift the pan from the heat.

Remove the skin and bones from the cooked fish

before breaking it into flakes. Put the flakes into the frying pan with the vegetables and spices, and stir well before transferring the contents of the pan to a mixing bowl. Now add the fresh coriander, lemon juice and mashed potatoes. Mix together gently so as to retain the texture and shape of the flakes of fish. Season to taste.

Shape the mixture into twenty to twenty-four small balls about 2.5 cm/1 inch in diameter. Dip them into the beaten egg and then coat in breadcrumbs. Deep-fry in hot fat for 3–5 minutes until golden brown, or bake in the oven as described above. Serve with a vegetable curry and brown rice or chapati.

HADDOCK AND CHEESE HOTPOT

An excellent variation on the fish pie theme. Serve with a salad or minted peas.

450g/1 lb haddock fillets, skinned
100g/4 oz mushrooms, sliced
40g/1½ oz butter
40g/1½ oz plain flour
275ml/½ pint milk
175g/6 oz Cheddar cheese, grated
½ onion, finely chopped
seasoning
2 medium potatoes, very thinly sliced
chopped parsley to garnish

Lay the haddock fillets in an ovenproof dish and scatter the sliced mushrooms over the top.

Melt the butter in a pan, stir in the flour and cook gently until the mixture begins to bubble. Remove from the heat and gradually add the milk, stirring well after each addition. Bring to the boil, stirring continuously until the sauce thickens. Stir in 150g/5 oz grated cheese and the chopped onion. Season well and pour over the fish.

Arrange the potato slices over the fish and sauce, making sure that they cover completely. Season, and top with the remaining cheese.

Bake in a preheated oven, gas mark 6 (200° C/400° F), for 50 minutes until golden brown on top and cooked through. Garnish with chopped parsley before serving.

SCOTTISH HADDOCK STEW

A very simple but nonetheless delicious way of serving fresh haddock.

450g/1 lb new potatoes, sliced
1 small bunch of spring onions, finely chopped
1 tbsp chopped fresh chives
1–2 tbsps chopped fresh parsley
seasoning
approx. 275ml/½ pint milk
approx. 275ml/½ pint water
450g/1 lb haddock fillets,
skinned and chopped into large pieces

Put a layer of potatoes in the bottom of a casserole-type pan. Cover with a layer of spring onion and sprinkle a little chopped chives and parsley on the top. Season to taste. Repeat the layers until all the vegetables have been used up. Barely cover with milk and water and bring to the boil. Cover and simmer gently for 10–15 minutes until the potatoes are barely tender. Place the fish on top, press down lightly to settle the potatoes and cover again. Reduce the heat and poach for 4–6 minutes until tender. Serve.

HADDOCK WITH DILL AND VEGETABLES

a knob of butter
2 onions, chopped
3 sticks of celery, chopped
4 leeks, thinly sliced
4 carrots, thinly sliced
1 tsp dill seeds
150ml/¼ pint dry white wine
350g/12 oz haddock fillets, skinned and chopped

Put all the ingredients, except for the haddock, in a pan and bring to the boil. Stir well, cover and then simmer gently for 10 minutes until the vegetables are barely tender. Add the fish, replace the lid and poach for 4–6 minutes more until that too is tender. Season to taste. Serve with boiled potatoes.

HADDOCK ROMAGNA

350g/12 oz haddock fillets, skinned
250g/9 oz lean bacon, thinly sliced
50g/2 oz Gruyère cheese, thinly sliced
wholewheat flour for dusting
2 eggs, beaten
100g/4 oz soft wholewheat breadcrumbs
50ml/2 fl. oz groundnut oil
50g/2 oz clarified butter

Cut the fish, across its breadth, into twelve even-sized pieces measuring 2.5–3.75 cm/1–1½ inches wide. Trim the bacon. Lay one slice of bacon on a chopping board, arrange a slice of fish across it and top with a slice of cheese. Then fold over the bacon so that the fish and cheese are sealed in an open ended 'parcel'. Repeat until all the remaining pieces of fish have been made into 'parcels'.

Carefully dip each 'parcel' first in flour, then beaten egg and finally into the breadcrumbs. Heat the oil and butter in a large frying pan and when the fat begins to bubble add the 'parcels'. The fat should come about halfway up each one. Fry over a moderate heat for 4–5 minutes on each side, turning down the heat if they brown too quickly. Drain on absorbent paper before serving.

LEMON HADDOCK CRISP

An old family recipe which I have taken from my grand-mother's recipe book. It tastes just as good now as it did when I was a child.

450g/1 lb haddock fillets
juice of 1 lemon
50–75g/2–3 oz soft wholewheat breadcrumbs
15g/½ oz butter

Skin the fillets and cut into pieces. Arrange in the bottom of an ovenproof dish. Pour over the lemon juice and sprinkle the breadcrumbs on top. Dot with butter and bake in a preheated oven, gas mark 5 (190° C/375° F), for 20–25 minutes until tender.

POACHED HADDOCK WITH MUSTARD BUTTER

50g/2 oz soft butter
2–3 tsps Dijon mustard
4 small haddock fillets, skinned
2 tbsps chopped fresh chives
approx. 425ml/¾ pint fish stock (p. 41)

Put the butter and mustard in a small bowl and cream together until smooth. Lay the fillets on a clean work surface and sprinkle half the chives over the top. Place a knob of mustard butter on each and fold the fish in half to cover it. Pat the remaining mustard butter into a rough rectangle and put into the refrigerator to firm up.

Pack the fish, side by side, in the bottom of a pan (there should be little room to spare) and barely cover with fish stock. Add the remaining chives and cover with a tightly fitting lid. Slowly bring to the boil and as soon as the stock begins to bubble remove the pan from the heat. Leave to stand for 6–8 minutes until the fish is tender. Carefully lift the fillets from the pan, using a slotted spoon or fish slice, and place on a warm serving dish. Cover and keep warm.

Bring the remaining stock in the fish pan to a fast boil and cook, uncovered, for several minutes. Meanwhile shape the firmed-up mustard butter into small balls or butter curls. Spoon 1 tablespoon stock over each fillet and arrange the butter shapes on top. The butter should just be beginning to melt as the dish is taken to the table.

HAKE

A member of the cod family which is becoming less common and more expensive as stocks dwindle. Hake is a white, tender, flaky fish that many consider superior to cod but only if it is eaten really fresh. Stale hake can be disappointingly insipid and woolly. There is one area, however, in which its supremacy over both the cod and the haddock is undisputed. Hake is one of the easiest fish to bone. Cooks love it because it becomes an ideal vehicle for stuffings, and it is equally popular with those who are appalled by the thought of finding a fish bone on their plate. Like cod, hake can be poached, baked, braised, grilled and fried.

HAKE PROVENÇAL

350g/12 oz tomatoes, chopped
1 small onion, chopped
1 clove of garlic, peeled and crushed
1 red pepper, thinly sliced
a pinch of dried marjoram
a pinch of dried oregano
a pinch of dried basil
freshly ground black pepper
4 hake fillets/steaks, skinned if necessary
10 black olives, stoned   juice of ½ lemon

Place half the chopped tomatoes, onion, garlic and red pepper in the bottom of an ovenproof dish. Sprinkle the herbs over the top and season with a little black pepper. Arrange the fish on top and cover with the remaining chopped vegetables. Scatter the olives over that and sprinkle with lemon juice. Cover and bake in a preheated oven, gas mark 5 (190° C/375° F), for 20 minutes until the fish is tender.

GLOUCESTER HAKE

675g/1½ lbs hake fillets/steaks, skinned if necessary
3 tbsps dry white wine
25g/1 oz butter
1 tbsp olive oil
1 clove of garlic, peeled and crushed
4 shallots, finely chopped
100g/4 oz button mushrooms, sliced
1 tbsp finely chopped fresh parsley
seasoning

Place the fish in a lightly oiled ovenproof dish. Pour over the wine. Bake in a preheated oven, gas mark 5 (190° C/375° F), for 20 minutes, basting occasionally.

Meanwhile melt the butter and oil in a small pan and sauté the garlic, shallots and button mushrooms for 4–5 minutes. When cooked place the fish on a serving dish and pour the cooking juices into the pan containing the mushrooms. Stir well before spooning the mushroom mixture over the fish. Sprinkle with parsley and season to taste before serving.

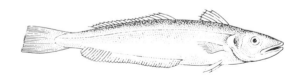

BAKED HAKE WITH CRUNCHY BREADCRUMBS

A light crunchy topping delicately flavoured with Cheddar cheese.

450–675g/1–1½ lbs hake fillets
40g/1½ oz butter
75g/3 oz soft wholewheat breadcrumbs
2 tbsps finely chopped fresh parsley
50g/2 oz Cheddar cheese, grated
freshly ground black pepper

Skin the fish and chop into pieces about 5 cm/2 inches long. Place in a lightly buttered ovenproof dish.

Melt the butter in a small pan, stir in the breadcrumbs and sauté for 3–4 minutes until they begin to crisp and brown. Spoon into a mixing bowl and stir in the parsley and grated cheese. Season to taste with black pepper. Sprinkle the topping over the hake and bake in a preheated oven, gas mark 5 (190° C/375° F), for 20 minutes.

SAFFRON CRUMBLE

A very popular dish, but one which I reserve for special occasions. It is not just the cost but the amount of fat used which makes me slightly reluctant to treat it as an everyday dish. Sometimes I replace the crumble topping with a light sprinkling of soft wholewheat breadcrumbs but I would be the first to admit that the original recipe tastes much better.

275ml/½ pint fish stock (p. 41)
a pinch of saffron strands
25g/1 oz butter
25g/1 oz unbleached white flour
450g/1 lb hake fillets
3 hard-boiled eggs, chopped
100g/4 oz prawns (optional)
1–2 tbsps chopped fresh parsley

FOR THE TOPPING
75g/3 oz wholewheat flour
25g/1 oz butter, diced
1 tbsp sunflower oil
50g/2 oz Cheddar cheese, grated
seasoning

Put the fish stock in a small pan with the saffron and bring to the boil. Simmer gently for 10 minutes. Melt the butter in a clean pan, stir in the flour and let the mixture bubble. Remove from the heat and gradually add the saffron stock, stirring well after each addition. Return to the heat and bring to the boil, stirring well, until the sauce thickens. Chop the hake into bite-sized pieces, removing any skin and bones, and stir into the sauce. Also add the eggs, prawns (if using them) and parsley. Spoon into an ovenproof dish.

To make the crumble topping, put the flour into a bowl and rub in the butter and oil. Stir in the grated cheese and season to taste. Sprinkle over the fish and bake in a preheated oven, gas mark 5 (190° C/375° F), for 20–25 minutes until golden brown.

HALIBUT

Halibut live in deep cold waters and rarely venture further south than Scotland. They can live for 60 years or so, in which time they grow to colossal sizes and can weigh up to 350 kg/770 lbs. I imagine that when they reach this size their flesh is rather unpalatable, but they are still highly prized, for halibut liver oil is one of the richest sources of Vitamin D. Such large fish are the exception rather than the rule and from a gastronomic point of view they are best around 1.5 kg/3¼ lbs. Baby halibut, known as chicken halibut in the trade, are even smaller.

Halibut used to be known as the workhouse fish but no-one is sure whether this was a term of contempt or simply a reference to the fact that one fully grown fish could feed a small army of people. Etymologists believe that the name has its roots in Scandinavia and means holy turbot. Certainly this is a much more accurate description of the fish's culinary qualities for it is generally considered to be on a par with the sole and turbot.

Halibut is one of my favourite fish and I am delighted to see that it is making an appearance on more and more fishmongers' slabs. It has firm, white flesh which is delicately flavoured. Larger fish are usually cut into steaks or cutlets and unless prepared carefully have a tendency to be dry. Those cut from the tail end of the fish are reputed to be worst in this respect. Smaller fish can be bought whole or filleted. They are best covered and baked or poached, and served with a sauce or moist garnish. Any recipe for sole or turbot can be used.

Halibut are available all year round but are best from August to April.

SEVICHE

Seviche or *ceviche* is a South American dish. Pieces of firm white fish are marinated in lime or lemon juice for up to 24 hours, during which time the acid 'cooks' the fish, turning it opaque like ordinary cooked fish. It is usually garnished with sweet peppers and served with bread as a tasty starter.

4 large lemons
4 spring onions, finely chopped
a liberal sprinkling of red chilli powder
freshly ground black pepper
450g/1 lb halibut fillets, skinned if necessary

Squeeze the lemons into a bowl and add the spring onions, chilli powder and black pepper. Cut the fish into small bite-sized cubes, removing any skin and bones, and toss into the bowl. Stir carefully. The lemon juice should barely cover the fish; add more if necessary.

Cover and leave in a cool place for 24 hours. Drain before serving.

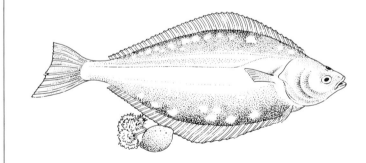

HALIBUT IN COCONUT SAUCE

3 tbsps fresh lime juice
1 tsp dried oregano
1 tsp dried dill weed
675g/1½ lbs halibut fillets, skinned and chopped
1 tbsp groundnut oil
1 small onion, chopped
approx. 275ml/½ pint fish stock (p. 41)
1 bay leaf
2 tbsps tomato purée
75g/3 oz block of creamed coconut, chopped
freshly ground black pepper
1 small red pepper, thinly sliced

Place 2 tbsps lime juice and half the dried oregano and dill weed in a small bowl and mix together well. Arrange the fish in a large shallow ovenproof dish and pour the lime juice marinade over it. Cover and leave in a cool place for 8–10 hours. Drain the fish and keep the liquid to use with the stock.

Heat the oil in a frying pan, add the onion and sauté until soft and golden. Put the marinade liquid into a measuring jug and add sufficient fish stock so that it measures 275ml/½ pint. Pour this liquid into the pan and add the bay leaf, the remaining oregano, dill weed and lime juice, the tomato purée and creamed coconut. Bring to the boil and cook gently, stirring frequently, until the creamed coconut has dissolved. Season to taste.

Pour the sauce over the fish and garnish with red pepper. Cover and bake in a preheated oven, gas mark 5 (190° C/375° F), for 20–25 minutes.

CREAMY CASSEROLED HALIBUT

2 leeks, thinly sliced
100g/4 oz button mushrooms, sliced
450g/1 lb halibut fillets, skinned
3–4 tomatoes, sliced
25g/1 oz butter
25g/1 oz unbleached white flour
275ml/½ pint fish stock (p. 41)
1 tbsp finely chopped fresh parsley
seasoning

Parboil or steam the leeks until they begin to soften. Put in the bottom of an ovenproof casserole dish and cover with the mushrooms. Lay the fillets on top (cut into pieces if necessary). Arrange the tomatoes over the fish.

To make the sauce, melt the butter in a pan and stir in the flour. Heat gently until the mixture begins to bubble. Remove from the heat and gradually add the fish stock, stirring well after each addition. Return to the stove and bring to the boil stirring well, until the sauce thickens. Add the parsley and season to taste. Pour over the tomatoes and bake in a preheated oven, gas mark 5 (190° C/375° F), for 20 minutes.

CIOPPINO

A fish stew which clearly has its roots in the Mediterranean but I came across it in a recipe booklet compiled by the fishermen's wives of Gloucester, Massachusetts on the Eastern Seaboard of North America.

1–2 tbsps olive oil
1 onion, chopped
1 clove of garlic, peeled and crushed
1 green pepper, chopped
1 carrot, chopped
1 stick of celery, chopped
450g/1 lb tomatoes, chopped
1 tbsp tomato purée (optional)
1 bay leaf
a good pinch of dried basil
a good pinch of saffron strands
150ml/¼ pint dry white wine
450g/1 lb halibut steaks
100g/4 oz shelled mussels
100g/4 oz peeled prawns

Heat the oil in a large, casserole-type pan, add the onion and garlic and sauté for 5–7 minutes until soft and golden. Add the remaining vegetables and continue to cook for 4–5 minutes, stirring frequently. Stir in the tomato purée (if using it), the bay leaf, dried basil, saffron and wine. Bring to the boil, cover and simmer gently for 15–20 minutes.

Meanwhile remove the skin and bones from the halibut and cut into bite-sized pieces. Add the main central bones (only those which can be fished out easily) to the stew.

When the vegetables are soft and have formed a rich stew remove the bay leaf and the fish bones. Add the hali-

but, cover, and simmer very gently for a further 3–4 minutes. Now place the mussels and prawns on top, replace the lid and cook for 4–5 minutes more until heated through. Serve with crusty bread.

BAKED HALIBUT EN PAPILLOTE

2 red peppers, sliced
4 halibut steaks
225g/8 oz button mushrooms, halved if necessary
25g/1 oz butter
4 sprigs of fresh parsley
seasoning

Cut four pieces of foil or greaseproof paper, each one being large enough to wrap around one of the halibut steaks. Arrange two to three slices of red pepper in the centre of each of the pieces of paper. Place the halibut steaks on top and cover with the remaining red pepper. Scatter the mushrooms over the top and dot with butter. Place a sprig of parsley on each and season to taste. Wrap the fish and vegetables in the paper, tucking the ends underneath, so that they are completely sealed inside four loose parcels and none of the cooking juices can escape. Put the parcels on a baking tray and bake in a preheated oven, gas mark 5 (190° C/375° F), for 20–25 minutes. Take care when unwrapping the fish to retain all the cooking juices inside the parcel and pour these over the fish before serving.

STIR-FRIED CHICKEN HALIBUT

A light and delicate dish which is equally good eaten as a starter or as a main course. Serve with brown rice or noodles. I use two types of soy sauce in cooking, and both are naturally fermented, containing no artificial additives: *shoyu* soy sauce is much lighter in flavour than *tamari* soy sauce, and is the one to use in this recipe as it allows the flavour of the fish and vegetables to come through.

450g/1 lb chicken halibut fillets, skinned
2 tbsps sesame oil
1 tbsp lemon juice
450g/1 lb courgettes, sliced
100g/4 oz button mushrooms, sliced
1–2 tbsps shoyu **soy sauce**

Cut the halibut into 2.5 cm/1 inch strips. Put into a small bowl and pour over 1 tablespoon sesame oil and the lemon juice. Mix together, cover and leave to marinate for 30 minutes.

Heat the remaining oil in a wok or large frying pan and stir-fry the courgettes for a minute or two. Toss in the mushrooms and cook for a minute or two more. When the courgettes are almost tender, drain the fish and add to the pan. Stir-fry for a minute before pouring over the soy sauce. Stir carefully and, when the fish is tender, serve.

HERRINGS

Fishing is fraught with dangers and catching the vast shoals of herrings which used to pass by our coastlines has cost many a brave man's life. In fairness to the herring, however, it must be said that it has probably saved many more from starvation.

Until over-fishing decimated stocks, herrings were cheap and plentiful and were eaten regularly by almost every family in the land. Only those living beside the sea ate them fresh, for they did not keep well and most were smoked, dried or salted before being sent to inland markets. Today almost anyone can eat fresh herrings and although they are not as plentiful as they were they are still reasonably cheap. They are at their best from mid-summer to late October but are generally available all the year round. Choose firm, plump fish whose eyes, gills and scales are bright and shiny.

Herrings are good sources of protein, iodine, Vitamins A and D and are rich in essential oils. They are best prepared in simple, time-honoured ways. Try dusting the fish with flour or semolina (the latter being a traditional way of cooking herrings in Norfolk) and place them in a hot, fairly heavy frying pan – no oil or fat is needed. Then, over a medium heat, cook for 7–10 minutes, turning once, until tender. The skin should be crisp and golden. Serve immediately with brown bread and butter or boiled potatoes. Fresh herrings can also be grilled or baked and served plain or with a variety of sauces; a mustard flavoured one being by far the most popular.

STUFFED HERRINGS CORNISH STYLE

50g/2 oz soft wholewheat breadcrumbs
4 soft herring roes
1 small onion, finely chopped
1 level tbsp finely chopped fresh sage
juice of ½ lemon
seasoning
4 herrings, filleted
150ml/¼ pint dry cider

Put the breadcrumbs, herring roe, onion, sage and lemon juice in a bowl and mix together well. Season to taste.

Divide the mixture into eight pieces and spread it over the narrow end of each herring fillet. Roll up the fillets, starting with the narrow end so that the filling is trapped inside. Arrange in a shallow ovenproof dish. The rolls can be secured with cocktail sticks or tied with cotton but I don't usually bother as, provided that the loose end of each roll is tucked underneath, it should not unfurl during cooking.

Pour over the cider and cover with foil. Bake in a pre-heated oven, gas mark 5 (190° C/375° F), for 25 minutes. Remove the foil and bake for a further 10 minutes until lightly browned.

GRILLED HERRINGS WITH MUSTARD SAUCE

425ml/¾ pint milk
½ carrot, sliced
2 slices of onion
5 black peppercorns
1 bay leaf
15g/½ oz butter
sunflower oil
25g/1 oz unbleached white flour
4 herrings
seasoning
2 tsps Dijon mustard

Put the milk, carrot, onion, peppercorns and bay leaf in a saucepan and bring to the boil. Remove from the heat and leave to stand for 15–20 minutes. Strain into a jug and wipe the pan clean.

Melt the butter and 1 tablespoon oil together in the pan and stir in the flour. Cook over a moderate heat for several minutes, letting the mixture bubble. Remove from the heat and gradually stir in the strained milk. Bring to the boil, stirring frequently, and cook until the sauce begins to thicken.

Meanwhile prepare the fish by removing the heads, tails and backbones (see page 24). Make two to three diagonal gashes in the sides of each fish and brush lightly with oil. Season well. Cook under a hot grill for 7–10 minutes, turning once, until tender. Just before serving stir the mustard into the white sauce and serve with the fish.

BAKED HERRINGS WITH RICE AND TOMATOES

This lunch or supper dish is both delicious and filling.

100g/4 oz long grain brown rice
a scant 275ml/½ pint water
1–2 tbsps olive oil
4 herrings, filleted
4–6 tomatoes, sliced
1–2 tbsps white wine vinegar
seasoning

Put the rice in a pan and pour over the water. Cover and bring to the boil. Simmer for 35–40 minutes, without stirring, until all the water has been absorbed and the rice is dry and tender.

Brush a shallow ovenproof dish with oil and lay the herring fillets in the bottom. Place half the tomatoes on top and sprinkle with wine vinegar. Season to taste. Spread the cooked rice over the top and cover with the remaining tomatoes. Brush the tomatoes with a little oil and bake in a preheated oven, gas mark 5 (190° C/375° F), for 25–30 minutes.

HERRINGS BAKED WITH CIDER

4 herrings
seasoning   1 onion, sliced
2 level tsps pickling spice
1 bay leaf
275ml/½ pint dry cider

Clean the fish and remove their heads, tails and backbones (see page 24). Cut each fish into two fillets. Season well and place a slice of onion on each fillet. Then roll up like a Swiss roll and pack into an ovenproof dish. Scatter the remaining onion, the pickling spices and bay leaf on top. Pour over the cider and bake in a preheated oven, gas mark 2 (150° C/300° F), for 1½ hours.

DEVILLED HERRINGS

A simple but effective way of serving herrings.

4 herrings
25g/1 oz butter, melted
1–2 tbsps Dijon mustard
white wine vinegar

Clean the fish and make two or three diagonal cuts on each side. Brush with some melted butter and place under a hot grill. Cook for 4–5 minutes on both sides.

Put the fish into an *au gratin* dish and paint with mustard. Pour over the remaining melted butter and sprinkle a drop or two of wine vinegar over each fish. Return to the hot grill and cook for a minute or two more before serving.

PASTA WITH HERRINGS

2 medium to large Florence fennel bulbs
50g/2 oz sultanas
450g/1 lb small herrings
2–3 tbsps olive oil
100g/4 oz pine kernels
450g/1 lb bucatini or spaghetti
4 tbsps thick-set natural yoghurt

Trim each fennel bulb and cut in half lengthways. Place in a pan of boiling water and cook for 5–6 minutes. Remove from the pan (reserve the cooking liquid) and drain well. Chop into small pieces. Soak the sultanas for 15 minutes or so in some of the water.

Clean each herring and remove the heads, tails and backbones (see page 24). Cut into strips and, with a sharp knife, ease the skin away from the flesh. Heat 1–2 tablespoons oil and lightly sauté the fish, breaking it up with a fork. Add the fennel, pine kernels, the drained sultanas and a little fennel water. Continue to cook gently for 5–10 minutes, adding more water if necessary but keep the mixture fairly dry.

Put the remaining cooking water in a large pan (adding more water if necessary) with 1 tablespoon of olive oil. Bring to a brisk boil and add the the pasta. Cook for 6–9 minutes until *al dente*.

Just before the pasta is ready stir the yoghurt into the fennel and herring mixture and season to taste. Heat through. Drain the pasta and place in a serving dish. Pour the fennel and herring mixture over the top and toss carefully. Serve with crusty bread and a green salad.

HERRINGS WITH DEVILLED ONIONS

4 herrings
sunflower oil
2 onions, chopped
150ml/¼ pint water
1 tbsp white wine vinegar
1–2 tsps Dijon mustard
seasoning

Clean the fish and remove their heads, tails and backbones (see page 24). Cook under a hot grill or in a hot, heavy frying pan for 7–10 minutes until tender.

While the fish are cooking heat a little oil in a pan and sauté the onions for 5–7 minutes until soft and golden brown. Pour in the water and wine vinegar. Bring to the boil and cook briskly until only 1–2 tablespoons of liquid remain. Stir in the mustard and season to taste. Serve with the herrings.

JOHN DORY

When seen from the side, the John Dory gives the impression of being a large, formidable fish. This illusion is shattered when viewed head on, for it is wafer-thin and has been described, very aptly, as plate-shaped. Its large head and wide prominent jaw has earned it the name of *l'horrible* in parts of France, but this is a little unfair. As a rule, revulsion soon turns to pity for the fish has such a doleful expression on its face that I, for one, can't help feeling sorry for it.

However, you are unlikely to come face to face with a John Dory for it is rarely displayed in our shops. It is not just a question of the fishmongers being protective of their customers' feelings for there is a marked absence of fillets too. I have always been told that 'there is no demand' but I have a growing suspicion that restaurateurs and hoteliers get there first. The John Dory is an ideal fish as far as they are concerned, ranked on a par with Dover sole, turbot and brill. Not only is the flavour excellent and the texture firm but it is also tolerant of a certain amount of overcooking and doesn't mind being kept waiting. In fact, it is becoming increasingly difficult to buy any of these fish from the fishmonger and I only wish professional chefs would be a little less greedy in their demands so that we too may have the pleasure of cooking and eating them.

The John Dory is expensive to buy not only because it is in demand but also because the head and viscera account for two-thirds of its total weight, and although four good fillets can be cut from each fish it is always necessary to buy more than usual. The leftovers, however, can be put to good use in stocks, soups and stews. Small fish can be used whole in soups such as *bouillabaisse* but it is more common to use the fillets. Cook them as for Dover sole, turbot and brill.

In most other European countries the John Dory is known as St Peter's fish, but it must not be confused with the freshwater fish of that name which is currently being imported into Britain from Israel. Like the haddock, John Dory has a golden-rimmed black spot behind each gill which is said to be the thumb print of St Peter. One story recounts how the fisherman saint caught one and was so moved by the fish's tearful expression that he threw it back into the water. Others claim that St Peter pulled the fish out of the Sea of Galilee at Christ's bidding and found in its mouth a coin which he was able to give to the money collectors who were pressing him for payment of temple taxes.

JOHN DORY WITH HERBS, CIDER AND CREAM

I found this excellent recipe in Alan Davidson's definitive work *North Atlantic Seafood* (Penguin, 1980). He, in turn, says that it is of Devonian origin and attributes it to a Mr and Mrs Milne from Dartmouth.

4 John Dory fillets (weighing approx. 75g/3 oz each)
seasoned flour
25g/1 oz butter
1 tbsp sunflower oil
chopped herbs (parsley; fennel leaves; marjoram or basil)
1 tbsp lemon juice
5–6 tbsps dry cider
2–3 tbsps single cream or top of the milk

Wash and dry the fillets, and dip them in seasoned flour. Heat the butter and oil in an enamelled skillet or pan (don't use metal because of the cider). Add the herbs and fillets and fry gently, skin side up, for 3–4 minutes. Then sprinkle the lemon juice over, add the cider, turn the heat right down, cover the fish and leave to simmer for 10 minutes.

Remove the skin from the fillets and add the cream to the small quantity of sauce in the dish. Serve the fish with their sauce straight from the pan with new potatoes and a green salad.

KIPPERS, *see* Smoked Fish

LANGOUSTINE, *see* Dublin Bay Prawns

LEMON SOLE

A very pleasant fish which is unfairly criticised by those who assume that it is related to the much-prized Dover sole. The lemon sole is not a sole at all but a member of the plaice family and although its flavour is comparable with that of the Dover sole its texture is much softer and the fish needs careful cooking. Provided that the cooking time is adjusted accordingly it can be used in any recipe calling for flat fish, including those for Dover sole. It is excellent egged, breadcrumbed and deep-fried, and is popular with children.

Lemon sole can be bought whole or filleted and is at its best from December to March.

LEMON SOLE WITH PURÉED LEEKS

The refreshing tang of the leek pureé complements the flavour of the fish perfectly but, to make the most of the combination, a little thought must be given to its presentation. Garnish lightly with chopped chives or a twist of lemon or, better still, serve it on brightly patterned plates.

450g/1 lb leeks
675g/1½ lbs lemon sole fillets, dark skin removed
juice of 1 lemon
2 level tsps Dijon mustard
seasoning

Trim, wash and thinly slice the leeks, then steam until tender. Cut the fish into four to six pieces and place in the bottom of a large ovenproof dish. Pour over the lemon juice and cover with foil. Bake in a preheated oven, gas mark 5 (190° C/375° F) for 8–12 minutes.

Meanwhile pass the leeks through a vegetable mouli or food processor and add the mustard. When the fish is tender drain off the cooking juices and stir into the puréed leeks. Season to taste. Return the fish to the oven to keep warm. Heat the purée and when hot serve with the fish.

LOBSTER

Lobsters are often thought of as being cardinal red but they only assume this colour after being cooked. When living in the sea they are a more discreet bluey/black. Lobster has always been something of a luxury food and is likely to remain so for the foreseeable future. Larger specimens, weighing around 3 kg/7 lbs, are the most economical buy but have not such a fine flavour as smaller ones. Generally speaking those weighing around 450–675g/1–1½ lbs are considered the sweetest. Available most of the year round, they are best in the summer months. Choose one that feels heavy for its size and if it is pre-cooked check that the tail springs back into a tight curl after being straightened out. Hen or female lobsters are broader around the tail than males and although their flesh isn't quite so delicately flavoured many people prefer them because of their bright red coral or roe.

There can be few people who enjoy cooking lobster and even fewer still who are prepared to cut them up while still alive, as directed in some recipes. The traditional method of plunging the lobster into boiling water or court-bouillon still seems to be the most popular and acceptable way of cooking lobster. From the moment the water reboils, cook a 450g/1 lb lobster for 15 minutes and a 675g/1½ lb one for 20 minutes.

More and more lobsters are being sold ready-boiled. All the customer has to do is dress it and savour its firm texture and delicate flavour with a little lemon juice and melted butter or mayonnaise. The meat can be reheated and served with any number of savoury sauces. Any leftovers can be used up in soups, salads and pâtés. I have had lobster curry but its fine flavour was somewhat drowned by the spices. A lobster weighing 450–675g/1–1½ lbs is sufficient for two people.

LOBSTER IN CHEESE SAUCE

A popular supper dish in Edwardian times.

Serves 2–3
1 cooked lobster, weighing 450–675g/1–1½ lbs
25g/1 oz butter
2 tbsps sunflower oil
50g/2 oz unbleached white flour
275ml/½ pint milk
275ml/½ pint court-bouillon (p. 40)
75g/3 oz Gruyère cheese, grated
2 tbsps grated Parmesan cheese

Shell the lobster and dice the meat (see pages 27–28). Put into the bottom of an *au gratin* dish. Melt the butter and oil in a pan and stir in the flour. Let the mixture bubble for a minute or two before removing from the heat. Gradually add the milk and court-bouillon, stirring well after each addition. Return to the heat and bring to the boil, stirring well, until the sauce thickens. Stir in the Gruyère cheese before pouring the sauce over the lobster. Sprinkle the Parmesan cheese on top and put under a hot grill until the sauce is beginning to brown and bubble. Serve with crusty bread and a salad.

SPECKLED LOBSTER

Serves 2–3
**1 cooked female lobster,
weighing 450–675g/1–1½ lbs
15g/½ oz butter
15g/½ oz unbleached white flour
175–200ml/6–7 fl. oz fish stock (p. 41)
½ onion, finely chopped
1 tbsp white wine vinegar**

Shell the lobster as described on pages 27–28. Chop the white meat into small pieces and keep aside with the coral.

Melt the butter in a pan and stir in the flour. Let the mixture bubble before removing from the heat. Gradually add 150ml/¼ pint fish stock, stirring well after each addition. Return to the heat and bring to the boil, stirring frequently, until the sauce begins to thicken. Remove from the heat once again and keep aside until needed.

Put the onion, wine vinegar and 2 tablespoons of fish stock in a clean pan and bring to the boil. Boil briskly until only 2 tablespoons of liquid remain. Strain and stir this into the sauce. Mash the coral and stir that into the sauce also. Put the chopped lobster meat into two or three small ramekin pots and pour over the sauce. Mix together. Bake in a preheated oven, gas mark 8 (230° C/450° F), for 10–12 minutes until the sauce is bubbling and the lobster is heated through.

MACKEREL

Grimod de la Reynière wrote (at the beginning of the nineteenth century, I hasten to add) that the 'mackerel has this in common with a good women – he is loved by all the world. He is welcomed by rich and poor with the same eagerness. He is most commonly eaten *à la maître d'hôtel*. But he may be prepared in a hundred ways; and he is as exquisite plain as in the most elaborate dressing.'

I find it hard to equate such sentiments with the mackerel on sale today. There is no doubt that it is a very handsome fish, its smooth, taut silvery-blue skin being mottled with iridescent greens and blues and patterned with black bands, but the flavour does not live up to expectations. In fact, it is rather too rich and strong for my palate and I only enjoy eating it in small amounts. Perhaps I would feel differently about the mackerel if I were able to eat it straight from the sea. My husband, who has spent a good deal of time aboard small boats, claims that this is the only way to eat mackerel – straight out of the water, into a hot pan and then on to the waiting plate.

Shakespeare and other writers of the time make many references to stinking mackerel and certainly the problem seems to have been much greater then than it is today. Mackerel are one of the oiliest fish and become rancid fairly quickly. Special measures were taken to try and ensure that they arrived at the markets in sound condition and they have the dubious distinction of being the only wet fish legally permitted to be sold on Sundays (but not for much longer if the Sunday Trading Bill passes through all its Parliamentary stages). It is important, even today, to choose fresh, bright-eyed fish as the flavour tends to become stronger and more pervasive the

older the fish. In quite a number of cookery books mackerel is described as tasting like trout and is said to have been known as poor man's trout. I must admit that the two fish have never struck me as having much in common and I would be far happier treating mackerel as if they were herrings than cooking them with almonds.

By far the best way to prepare small fresh mackerel is to dry fry or grill them; larger ones are good stuffed and baked. There seems to be some disagreement as to whether mackerel should be cooked in a liquid, be it wine, court-bouillon, cider or water. Some cooks claim that it ruins the flavour of the fish while others cite delicious mackerel soups from Sweden and recipes for Cornish marinated mackerel baked in vinegar or cider. The two classic ways of serving mackerel are with gooseberry sauce or with a good *beurre maître d'hôtel* (butter mixed with lemon juice and parsley).

Smoked mackerel is discussed in the Smoked Fish section.

STUFFED MACKEREL

4 small mackerel
1 small onion, finely chopped
1 small eating apple, grated
1 grapefruit
2 tbsps fresh parsley, finely chopped
a good 50g/2 oz soft wholewheat breadcrumbs
seasoning
1 tbsps sunflower oil

Trim the fins from the fish and remove the gills. Slit each fish open along the backbone, work the bone loose and then cut it free where it joins the neck and tail. Discard, taking the viscera with it. Wash the fish and pat dry carefully.

To make the stuffing, put the onion and apple in a mixing bowl. Peel the grapefruit, removing the white pith, and chop the flesh into small pieces, discarding pips and any tough pieces of membrane. Put the chopped grapefruit and as much of the juice as possible into the bowl. Stir in the parsley and breadcrumbs and season to taste. Fill the mackerel with the stuffing and lightly brush with oil. Place the fish in the bottom of an ovenproof dish, packed fairly close together so that they don't fall over. Bake in a preheated oven, gas mark 5 (190° C–375° F), for 20–25 minutes.

Facing page 96: Stuffed Mackerel (above).
Left: Haddock and Cheese Hotpot (page 81); photograph courtesy of the Milk Marketing Board.

MACKEREL WITH TOMATOES

2 leeks, sliced
2 sticks of celery, chopped
6 tomatoes, chopped
4 tbsps water
1–2 tbsps finely chopped fresh parsley
seasoning
1 tbsp sunflower oil
2–3 mackerel, filleted

Put the leeks, celery, tomatoes and water in a pan and bring to the boil. Cover and simmer for 10–15 minutes until the vegetables have begun to soften and most of the water has evaporated away. Boil briskly to reduce if necessary. Add the parsley and season to taste.

Lightly brush a shallow ovenproof dish with oil and arrange the fish in the bottom, skins downwards. Spoon the vegetable mixture over the top and bake in a pre-heated oven, gas mark 5 (190° C/375° F), for 20 minutes. Serve with boiled potatoes or brown rice.

MACKEREL WITH MELTED BUTTER AND PARSLEY SAUCE

The simple but effective sauce of this recipe can be served with almost any type of fish.

4 small mackerel
50g/2 oz butter, melted
juice of 1 lemon
1 tbsp finely chopped fresh parsley

Cut off the heads, tails and fins of the mackerel. Clean thoroughly and rinse well before patting dry. Make two to three diagonal cuts in both the sides of each fish and brush with melted butter. When all the fish are prepared in this way cook under a hot grill for 4–6 minutes, then turn over and cook the other side for a similar period.

Just before the fish are ready heat the remaining butter. Add a drop or two of cold water, the lemon juice and parsley. Stir well. Arrange the cooked fish on a hot serving dish and pour over the butter·sauce. Serve immediately while sizzlingly hot.

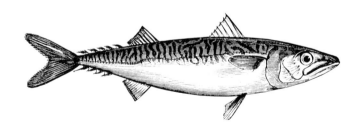

MARINATED MACKEREL WITH FENNEL

This recipe comes from Arabella Boxer's book, *Cooking with Herbs* (Octopus Books, 1980). As with most of her recipes it is both unusual and exceedingly good. I sometimes take the liberty of substituting yoghurt for the soured cream.

2 medium mackerel
6 tbsps soured cream
a pinch of dry mustard
seasoning
yolks of 2 hard-boiled eggs
1 tbsp chopped fennel or dill leaves

FOR THE MARINADE
275ml/½ pint dry white wine
4 tbsps white wine vinegar
1 shallot, chopped
1 clove of garlic, peeled and crushed
1 bay leaf
6 black peppercorns
3 stalks of celery, chopped
2 sprigs of fresh thyme

Clean the mackerel, remove the heads and tails and place the fish in a large pan. Put all the ingredients for the marinade in a small pan and bring to the boil. Cook for 20 minutes, then pour it over the mackerel. Bring to the boil, cover and simmer for about 10 minutes. Leave the fish to cool in the marinade, then lift them out and cut them into eight thin fillets, free from all skin and bone. Lay them in a shallow dish.

To make the sauce mix the soured cream with 2 tablespoons of the strained marinade in a bowl and add the mustard and seasoning. Beat until smooth and pour over the fillets.

Chop the egg yolks and scatter them evenly over the dish. Chop the fennel (or dill) leaves and sprinkle them all over. Chill for an hour or two before serving. Serve with brown bread and butter.

MONKFISH (ANGLER FISH)

Fishmongers are reluctant to give their customers so much as a glimpse of the monkfish, fearing that it may affect their sensibilities. Indeed, it is an ugly fish, shaped rather like a huge tadpole with a large bulbous head and fleshy tail. Only the tail is eaten, cut into varying sizes from thin steaks to large joints. The brown skin is always removed to reveal a delicate pink flesh which whitens during cooking. It is firm, succulent and 'meaty'; in France it is known as *gigot de mer*, and some cooks even suggesting roasting a large tail piece as if it were indeed a leg of lamb. There are no small bones to worry about, just a central cartilaginous spine. Whenever possible choose a thick middle cut for the tail becomes noticeably 'bonier' towards the tip.

Monkfish are fairly common in our coastal waters but you wouldn't think so judging by the infrequency with which they appear in our shops. The flavour and texture are more like those of shellfish, and in the past the flesh has been used as a substitute for the more expensive lobster and scallop. While there is nothing wrong with cooking monkfish thermidor or monkfish St Jacques it would be a pity not to give the monkfish the credit it so richly deserves. It can be grilled, fried, braised or poached and its excellent flavour marries well with most of the classic sauces.

MONKFISH CASSEROLE

1–2 tbsps sunflower or groundnut oil
2 mild onions, chopped
1 green pepper, sliced
450g/1 lb tomatoes, chopped
4 potatoes, sliced
1–2 tbsps tomato purée (optional)
approx. 575ml/1 pint fumet/fish stock (p. 41)
seasoning
675g/1½ lbs monkfish, roughly chopped

Heat the oil in a large pan, add the onions and sauté for 5–7 minutes until they begin to soften. Add the green pepper and the tomatoes and cook for 2–3 minutes more before adding the potatoes. Stir in the tomato purée (if using it) and barely cover the vegetables with fish stock. Season to taste. Cover and simmer gently until potatoes are almost tender. Add the fish and cook for a further 5–10 minutes until that too is tender. Serve with granary bread and a green salad or vegetable.

MONKFISH TART

175g/6 oz wholewheat flour
75g/3 oz butter, diced
a good pinch each of dried thyme, marjoram, oregano and basil
1 tbsp finely chopped fresh parsley
1 tsp English mustard
6 tsps cold water

FOR THE FILLING
225g/8 oz monkfish
1–2 tbsps sunflower oil
1 onion, chopped
100g/4 oz button mushrooms, chopped
40g/1½ oz butter
50g/2 oz unbleached white flour
200ml/7 fl. oz milk
2 egg yolks
2 good tbsps natural yoghurt
½ level tsp ground mace
freshly ground black pepper

To make the pastry, put the flour in a bowl and rub in the butter until the mixture resembles breadcrumbs. Stir in the dried and fresh herbs and mustard. Add the water and mix to form a pastry dough. Turn out onto a floured board and roll out. Line a 20 cm/8 inch flan ring. Prick the pastry base with a fork and bake blind in a preheated oven, gas mark 6 (200° C/400° F), for 10 minutes.

Remove the bones from the monkfish and chop into small pieces. Heat the oil in a pan, add the onion and sauté for 5–7 minutes. Add the monkfish and mushrooms and cook for another 5 minutes. Remove with a slotted spoon and place in the bottom of the blind-baked pastry case.

Melt the butter in the pan, stir in the flour and cook

until the mixture begins to bubble. Remove from the heat and gradually add the milk, stirring well after each addition. Return to the heat and cook gently, stirring frequently, until the sauce becomes fairly thick. Beat the egg yolks and yoghurt together and stir almost all the mixture (keep back 2 tablespoons to use as a glaze) into the sauce. Season with mace and black pepper. Pour over the monkfish. Brush the top of the tart with the remaining egg and yoghurt mixture and return to the oven. Bake for 25 minutes until golden brown. Serve warm or cold.

MONKFISH WITH ARTICHOKES

The globe artichoke is one of my favourite vegetables. For those of you unfamiliar with its light subtle flavour I suggest that before you try this recipe you eat one on its own, accompanied by nothing stronger then melted butter. Simply trim the stalk and remove any damaged or tough-looking leaves and cook for 40–45 minutes in a large pan of boiling water to which you have added the juice of a half lemon.

Once cooked, each tender leaf (strictly speaking we should call them petals) is plucked from the head, the fleshier root end is dipped in butter and then gently nibbled and sucked to remove the delicate flesh. The best part, the heart, lies at the base of each artichoke and is gradually uncovered as each layer of leaves is pulled away, eaten and discarded. Even when the last leaf has been removed the heart still lies hidden beneath a thistle-like down or 'choke' which has to be scooped away before the heart can be savoured.

This recipe brings out the best in both the monkfish and the globe artichoke but it isn't necessary to use grade one artichokes which are always expensive. Try to find small, slightly marked ones which will be cheaper. I generally serve this dish as a first course or as a luncheon dish for two.

3 globe artichokes
juice of 1 lemon
350g/12 oz monkfish
2–3 tbsps olive oil
150ml/¼ pint dry white wine
seasoning

Trim one artichoke at a time, remembering to rub each cut with lemon juice to prevent the flesh discolouring. First cut off the stalk close to the head. Remove all the tough outer leaves, and slice off the top about half way up the head and discard. You should be left with the bottom half of the artichoke which must now be cut in half from top to bottom. Remove the hairy choke with a sharp knife. Thinly slice the remaining artichoke. Repeat until all the artichokes have been prepared in this fashion. Cut the monkfish into delicate slices too.

Heat the oil in a large frying pan, add the artichokes and sauté for 4–5 minutes, stirring frequently. Add the fish and brown on both sides. Pour over the wine, letting it bubble before reducing the heat. Cook for a minute or two more to ensure that both the artichokes and the fish are tender, by which time most of the wine will have disappeared. Season to taste and serve with fresh bread.

CREAM OF MONKFISH SOUP

Serves 4–6

FOR THE FUMET/STOCK
1.5 litres/2½ pints water
675g/1½ lbs fish trimmings
2 small gurnard, cleaned
1 onion, chopped
1 carrot, chopped
1 sprig of fresh parsley
1 sprig of fresh thyme
1 bay leaf
10 black peppercorns

FOR THE SOUP
225g/8 oz monkfish
75g/3 oz butter
50g/2 oz unbleached white flour
150ml/¼ pint soured cream
2 egg yolks   2 tsps lemon juice

Put the ingredients needed to make the stock in a large pan. Cover and bring to the boil. Simmer for 30 minutes. Strain, pushing through as much of the soft fish and vegetable mixture as you wish. Return the fumet/stock to the pan. Add the monkfish and poach for 5–8 minutes until cooked. Put into a liquidiser or food processor and process until smooth. Pass through a sieve into a clean pan. Heat through.

Work the butter and flour together to form a *beurre manié*. Divide into small balls and stir into the hot broth, one at a time. Cook gently over a low to moderate heat until the soup begins to thicken. Beat the soured cream and egg yolks together and stir into the soup. Heat through gently, taking care not to boil, and then add lemon juice to taste.

MUSSELS

In Britain at least, mussels are not very popular and tend to be regarded as the poor relations of lobsters, scallops, crabs and prawns. This is a pity for they are cheap, readily available, highly nutritious and well flavoured. Buy them from reputable sources to ensure that they are fresh and have been collected from unpolluted waters.

Mussels require very little cooking and, contrary to popular belief, are easy to prepare provided that they are relatively clean in the first place. This may seem to be a contradiction of terms but the principal disadvantage of mussels compared to many other shellfish is that they often harbour small pieces of grit and sand which can prove difficult to remove. These days most mussels spend time in cleansing tanks before they find their way into the shops and the problem is not as great as it used to be. However, occasionally one or two seem to slip through the net. It is virtually impossible to tell whether a mussel is clean or not simply by looking at it, and one must take pot luck although I do tend to steer clear of mussels whose shells are covered with barnacles and seaweed.

When I first started using shellfish I was very confused by recipes referring to pints of mussels as they are now sold by the pound (weight). I have since discovered the origin of the old measure: years ago when barrow boys and street hawkers did not own proper weighing scales they simply used their empty beer mugs as a measure.

Recipes for mussels range from the relatively simple and yet delicious *moules marinière* in which the mussels are cooked with wine, shallots and parsley (recipe on page 105) to the more elaborate and dramatic Middle Eastern dish of stuffed mussels (see page 103). Mussels can also be used in soups, paellas, risottos, salads and pies.

Mussels are also available smoked, and I discuss them in the Smoked Fish section.

STUFFED MUSSELS

I first came across the idea of stuffing mussel shells in Tess Mallo's excellent book, *The Complete Middle Eastern Cook Book* (Summit, 1980). The method is fairly straightforward although it does require a fair amount of time and patience on the part of the cook. The results however certainly justify the effort and are not only extremely tasty but are also very impressive.

1.3kg/3 lbs mussels
275ml/½ pint dry white wine
4–5 tbsps finely chopped fresh parsley
1–2 tbsps olive oil
2 onions, finely chopped
75g/3 oz cashews, chopped
225g/8 oz long grain brown rice
seasoning

Clean the mussels throughly, removing their beards and discarding any that are already open. Put the mussels in a large pan with the wine and 1 tablespoon of chopped parsley. Bring to the boil, cover and cook for 2–4 minutes, shaking the pan regularly, until most of the shells have opened. Discard those that remain closed. When cool enough to handle lift them from the pan, one at a time, and, without opening them further, scoop out the fleshy mussel. Chop each mussel in half and keep aside until needed. Keep the empty shells and cooking stock aside too.

Heat the oil in another pan. Add the onions and sauté for 5–7 minutes until soft and golden. Toss in the cashews and sauté them until they begin to brown lightly. Add the rice and stir-fry for 2–3 minutes. Line a sieve with damp butter muslin and strain the cooking stock into a measuring jug. Add sufficient water to make the amount up to 275ml/½ pint and pour over the rice. Bring to the boil, cover and simmer gently for 15–20 minutes, without stirring, until all the liquid has been absorbed and the rice is dry. Stir in the chopped mussels and the remaining parsley. Season to taste.

When the rice mixture is cool enough to handle spoon 1–2 teaspoons into each empty shell. Press the two halves of the shell together as if to close, and arrange in the bottom of a large pan. Pack the shells close together so that the rice mixture does not spill out. Pour over 275ml/½ pint water. Place a large flat plate on top of the mussels and stand a heavy kitchen weight on top of that. Bring the water to the boil, cover and simmer for 20–25 minutes until all the water has been absorbed. The rice should be dry and tender. Remove the pan from the heat and leave to cool.

When cool remove the lid, weight and the plate and lift out the mussels. Rub each shell carefully with a lightly oiled cloth to make them gleam. Serve cold with pitta bread and a selection of side salads.

MUSSEL SOUP

A smooth and colourful soup which enables everyone, even those who are reluctant to eat mussels because of their appearance, to enjoy their wonderful flavour.

Serves 4–6
1kg/2–2¼ lbs mussels
1 onion, finely chopped
1 sprig of fresh parsley
275ml/½ pint dry white wine
50g/2 oz butter
2 tbsps unbleached white flour
575ml/1 pint milk
freshly ground black pepper

Wash and scrub the mussels thoroughly, remove the beards and discard any that are open. Put them in a large pan with the chopped onion, parsley and wine. Cover and bring to the boil. Cook for about 3–5 minutes, shaking the pan frequently, until most of the shells have opened. Strain and reserve the stock, and discard any mussels which have not opened. When cool enough to handle remove the mussels from the opened shells.

Heat the butter in another pan and stir in the flour. Let the mixture bubble for a minute or two, stirring to prevent it burning. Remove from the heat and add the milk, a little at a time, stirring well after each addition. Return to the heat and bring to the boil, stirring until the sauce begins to thicken. Strain the mussel stock through a sieve lined with muslin, and then pour into the sauce and heat through. Finely chop the mussels and stir them into the soup. Season with black pepper and heat through. Don't boil the soup once the mussels have been added or they will become rather rubbery.

MUSHROOMS STUFFED WITH MUSSELS

4 large flat mushrooms
100g/4 oz button mushrooms
100g/4 oz shelled mussels, chopped
2–3 tbsps finely chopped fresh parsley
grated rind of 1 lemon
2 eggs, beaten
freshly ground black pepper
50g/2 oz soft wholewheat breadcrumbs
a knob of butter

Wipe all the mushrooms clean and then remove the stalks from the large flat mushrooms. Finely chop these stalks and the button mushrooms and put them into a mixing bowl. Stir in the mussels, parsley, grated lemon rind and beaten eggs. Season to taste with black pepper.

Place the large flat mushrooms in a buttered ovenproof dish and spoon the mussel mixture over the top. Sprinkle with the breadcrumbs and dot with butter. Bake in a pre-heated oven, gas mark 4 (180° C/350° F), for 10–15 minutes. Serve on hot buttered toast.

ARROZ CON MEJILLONES
(Rice with mussels)

A traditional Spanish dish that is both colourful and flavoursome.

1–2 tbsps olive oil
3–4 cloves of garlic, peeled and crushed
275g/10 oz long grain brown rice
725ml/1¼ pints water
a good pinch of saffron strands
3–4 tbsps finely chopped fresh parsley
225g/8 oz shelled mussels
10 black olives, stoned
seasoning

Heat the oil in a heavy pan, add the garlic and rice, and sauté for 3–4 minutes until the rice begins to look translucent. Pour over the water and stir in the saffron and 2 tablespoons of the parsley. Bring to the boil, cover and simmer for 30 minutes without stirring.

Lay the mussels and olives on top of the rice and replace the lid. Cook for a further 5–10 minutes until all the water has been absorbed and the rice is dry and tender.

Remove from the heat and stir carefully. Season to taste and sprinkle with the remaining parsley before serving.

MOULES MARINIÈRE

A popular dish which appears regularly on restaurant menus. It deserves to be made more often in the family kitchen for it is inexpensive, quick and easy to prepare.

Serves 4–6
2.25kg/5 lb mussels
1 onion, chopped
2 cloves of garlic, peeled and crushed
1 sprig of fresh parsley
1 sprig of fresh thyme
275ml/½ pint dry white wine
2 tbsps finely chopped fresh parsley
seasoning

Scrub the mussels under cold running water and scrape any barnacles from the shells. Pull away the hairy beards and discard any mussels which are open. Put the cleaned mussels into a large pan with the onion, garlic, herb sprigs and the wine. Bring to the boil and cover with a tight fitting lid. Cook for 2–3 minutes, shaking the pan occasionally until most of the mussels have opened. Remove from the heat. Stand a sieve over a large bowl and tip the content of the pan into it. Pull away and discard the top shell of each mussel. Throw away any mussels that have not opened.

Rinse the pan. Line a sieve with damp butter muslin and stand over the pan. Pour the stock from the bowl through the sieve into the pan. Then bring to a slow boil and toss in the mussels, still attached to the bottom shells. Cook for 1–2 minutes before removing with a slotted spoon. Put them into individual serving dishes. Strain the stock through the lined sieve for a second time and then pour over the mussels. Sprinkle with chopped parsley and serve with crusty bread.

SPAGHETTI WITH MUSSELS

2 tbsps olive oil
1 onion, chopped
1 clove of garlic, peeled and crushed
1 red pepper, chopped
675g/1½ lbs ripe tomatoes, chopped
2–3 tbsps finely chopped fresh parsley
seasoning
350g/12 oz shelled mussels
450g/1 lb spaghetti

Heat 1 tablespoon oil in a frying pan and sauté the onion and garlic until soft and golden. Add the red pepper and the tomatoes and cook gently until the tomatoes are very soft and reduced to a virtual purée. If the sauce becomes too thick add a dash of wine or water. Stir in the parsley and season to taste. Add the mussels, cover and cook gently for 4–5 minutes until heated through.

Meanwhile bring a large pan of water to the boil, add the remaining oil and the pasta. Bring to the boil and cook until the pasta is *al dente*. Drain well and put into a serving dish. Pour over the hot sauce and serve immediately.

SEAFOOD SAFFRON RICE

1.3kg/3 lbs mussels
150ml/¼ pint dry white wine
1 sprig of fresh parsley
2–3 tbsps olive oil
1 onion, chopped
225g/8 oz long grain brown rice
approx. 425ml/¾ pint fish stock (p. 41) or water
a good pinch of saffron strands
4 small to medium squid
100g/4 oz peeled prawns
1 tbsp chopped fresh parsley
seasoning
100g/4 oz prawns in their shells

Scrub the mussels well, remove the beards and discard any that are open. Put into a large pan and pour the wine over them. Add the sprig of parsley and cover with a tight fitting lid. Bring to the boil and cook over a fairly high heat, shaking the pan frequently for 3–5 minutes, until most of the shells have opened. Discard any that have not. Remove and discard the shells from three-quarters of the cooked mussels. Line a sieve with muslin and stand over a bowl. Strain the cooking stock into the bowl. Keep all the mussels and the strained stock aside until needed.

Heat 1 tablespoon oil in a heavy pan, add the onion and sauté until soft and golden. Add the rice and continue to cook, stirring frequently, for a further 3–4 minutes. Add sufficient fish stock or water to the strained stock to make the amount up to 575ml/1 pint and pour over the rice. Sprinkle the saffron over the top and bring to the boil. Cover and simmer for 35–40 minutes, without stirring, until all the water has been absorbed and the rice is tender and dry.

Meanwhile prepare the squid as directed on page 25. Chop the tentacles and triangular fins and slice the bag-like bodies into 6 mm/¼ inch rings. Heat another table-spoon of oil in a frying pan and toss in the squid. Sauté for 3–4 minutes and then put into the pan containing the cooked rice. Also add the peeled prawns, shelled mussels and chopped parsley. Mix together carefully and season to taste. Spoon the mixture into a shallow ovenproof dish. Arrange the unshelled prawns and mussels on top of the rice and cover with foil. Place in a preheated oven, gas mark 5 (190° C/375° F) for 15–20 minutes until heated through. Serve with a green salad and crusty bread.

NORWAY LOBSTER, *see* Dublin Bay Prawns

OCTOPUS

Some fishmongers, in an attempt to make the octopus look more appealing, sell it ready cleaned and skinned while others sell only the tentacles. Mine has struck a pleasing balance for he simply removes the grey blue skin revealing the more appetising white meat. Octopuses vary in size but it is worth remembering that the larger the specimen the longer it will take to cook. With very large octopuses only the tentacles are worth eating and even then I suggest that you beat them well with a rolling pin or steak tenderizer. Greek fishermen are reputed to bash each octopus 99 times against a rock before selling

them! The most tender succulent flesh is found on those octopus which are less than 37.5 cm/15 inches long. Like the other members of the cephalopod family, octopus can be prepared in many ways but unless they are very small they are best stewed gently until tender.

A recent attraction at my local pub has been tiny pickled octopus. Unfortunately they proved so popular that by the time I arrived the large glass jar was empty!

NEW ENGLAND OCTOPUS

2 octopuses (weighing 450g/1 lb each)
2–3 tbsps olive oil
2 onions, sliced
2 cloves of garlic, peeled and crushed
juice of 1 lemon
425ml/¾ pint water
2–3 tbsps chopped fresh parsley
seasoning

Prepare the octopus as shown on page 26. Cut into bite-sized pieces. Heat the oil in a heavy, casserole-type pan, add the octopus, onions and garlic and sauté for 5–7 minutes. Pour over the lemon juice and water, stir in the parsley and season to taste. Bring to the boil, cover and simmer gently for 35–40 minutes until the octopus is almost tender. Uncover and boil briskly for 10 minutes to reduce and thicken the stock. Serve with wholewheat spaghetti.

CASSEROLED OCTOPUS WITH VEGETABLES AND ROSEMARY

Although not as flamboyant or dramatic as some recipes, this can be a positive advantage, for not everyone is enthusiastic or confident about preparing or eating deep-fried whole baby octopus or octopus cooked in their own ink. This recipe has a much more homely appeal and I can recommend it to anyone who is about to cook octopus for the first time.

2 octopuses (weighing 450g/1 lb each)
3–4 tbsps olive oil
3 cloves of garlic, peeled and crushed
4 sticks of celery, chopped
4 carrots, diced
4 potatoes, diced
2–3 tbsps tomato purée
2 tbsps white wine vinegar
juice of 1 lemon
575ml/1 pint water
2 sprigs of fresh rosemary, finely chopped
freshly ground black pepper

Prepare the octopus as shown on page 26. Chop into bite-sized pieces. Heat the oil in a large casserole-type pan, add the octopus and sauté for 3–4 minutes. Add the garlic, celery, carrots and potatoes and fry for several minutes more. Add the remaining ingredients and bring to the boil. Cover and simmer for 45–55 minutes until the octopus is tender. Octopuses larger than those suggested in the recipe will take longer to cook, perhaps up to 2 hours, and more water may need to be added to the pan.

OYSTERS

Man has been eating oysters since Neolithic times but never more than in the eighteenth and nineteenth centuries when they were abundant and cheap. Dr Johnson was able to feed his cat, Hodge, on them for two pence a day, and they became associated with the poor in Dickensian days. *The Times Telescope* reported in 1832 that 'on St James' Day [July 25] large quantities of oysters were eaten by Londoners, but their children were content to use the shells for building miniature grottos and to illuminate these by means of rush lights. The children ask passers-by for contributions to the grottos. This is an annual custom, but it lasts for several weeks, to the annoyance of pedestrians.' Apparently the more oysters you could eat on St James' Day the better; for it was said that provided you ate generously you would not want for money during the year. A dozen oysters and a pint of this or that was also said to mellow the soul, banish melancholy and ward off beri-beri!

When oysters began to become scarce in the mid-nineteenth century Europe was taken by surprise and one French gourmet wrote, 'oysters seem to be losing ground this year. It can't be more than a breathing spell, a bad joke of fortune.' Unfortunately the truth was that the natural oyster beds had been stripped clean and the heyday of the oyster was gone forever. Since then great strides have been made in oyster farming and they are still available but at a wicked price.

The traditional way, and many people would say the only way, to eat oysters is straight from the shell with a drop or two of lemon juice. Some people recommend biting into the flesh to release the flavour in the liver before slipping the oyster down the gullet. Once open, place the oyster and its liquid in the deepest of the two shells. The shells can be steadied by placing them on a bed of cracked ice. Serve with thin slices of buttered brown bread and lemon juice. Some people claim that the meal isn't complete without a glass of champagne while others prefer to eat their oysters with Guinness.

When oysters were two a penny they were added to steak and kidney pies, made into soups and stews and used in a hundred and one different ways. Hardly anyone bothers to cook them these days, as they are simply too expensive, but if you should be tempted remember to cook them briefly, just until the edges begin to curl.

ANGELS ON HORSEBACK

A traditional after-dinner savoury which is equally good served as an hors d'oeuvre.

8–12 oysters
8–12 thin rashers of plain bacon, trimmed

Remove the oysters from their shells as described on pages 26–27. Rinse lightly and pat dry. Wrap a rasher of bacon around each oyster and put onto oiled skewers. Grill until the bacon is crisp. Serve on triangles of buttered wholewheat toast.

POACHED OYSTERS WITH VELOUTÉ SAUCE

8–12 oysters
15g/½ oz butter
15g/½ oz unbleached white flour
150ml/¼ pint fish stock/fumet (p. 41)
1 tbsp dry white wine
1 tbsp finely chopped fresh parsley

Open the oysters carefully so as not to spill any of the liquid inside each shell. See pages 26–27 for instructions. Tip the oysters and their liquid into a pan. Cover and leave aside until needed.

To make the sauce, melt the butter in a small pan, stir in the flour and cook gently, letting the mixture bubble. Remove from the heat and add the stock and wine, a little at a time, stirring well after each addition. Return to the heat and bring to the boil, stirring continuously, until the sauce thickens.

Bring the pan containing the oysters to a very slow boil and poach for 1–2 minutes. Lift the poached oysters from the pan with slotted spoon and place one in each of the deepest shells. Cover with a little of the sauce and sprinkle the top with parsley. Serve immediately.

BAKED OYSTERS

**8–12 oysters
juice of ½–1 lemon
25–50g/1–2 oz soft wholewheat breadcrumbs
½–1 tsp cayenne pepper
25g/1 oz butter**

Remove the oysters from their shells as described on pages 26–27. Rinse lightly and pat dry. Place one oyster in each deep shell. Sprinkle a few drops of lemon juice, some breadcrumbs and a small pinch of cayenne pepper over each oyster. Dot with butter and stand the shells on a baking tray. Bake in a preheated oven gas mark 8 (230° C/450° F) for 5–10 minutes, or brown under a hot grill.

PILCHARDS

The pilchard's Latin name, *sardina pilchardus*, suggests that it has more in common with the sardine than meets the eye. Waverely Root says of it, 'a name adopted by certain European fish when they decide they have become too old to be put up with being called sardines'. Indeed pilchards are mature sardines. They are fairly oily fish and do not travel well. You are unlikely to find fresh ones away from the warm seas off the Cornish coast, the Bay of Biscay and the Mediterranean. They can be scaled, gutted and grilled or dry-fried until crisp and tender and, like sardines, they are excellent served cold in salads and hors d'oeuvres.

A traditional Cornish dish, using local pilchards, is star-gazey pie. The gutted fish were arranged, like the spokes of a wheel, in a deep pie dish with their tails curled round a central pie funnel and their heads resting on the lip of the dish. Chopped hard-boiled eggs or onions were then scattered over the fish before the whole thing was topped with pastry and baked. As the pastry crisped and browned so too did the exposed fish heads which meant that they could be easily snipped off before the pie was taken to the table. On the face of it this seems a strange way to make a fish pie but there was sound reasoning behind it. The head of the pilchard contains a lot of goodness and flavour and by baking the fish whole the valuable oils and juices seeped down into the pie. It is still good advice although I imagine most of us today are rather more squeamish than we are frugal.

PLAICE

Plaice is the best known and most commercially important flat fish. It is particularly well suited to living on the sand bars of the North Sea. The warm brown colouring of its back, speckled with rust-coloured spots, keep it camouflaged and hidden from predators and it is said to 'move across the seabed like a billowing magic carpet'. Its distinctive shape has resulted in it being nicknamed 'diamond plaice' on the South coast.

Plaice is used widely by restaurants, fish and chip shops and in the home but, unfortunately, as with so many things, familiarity has bred contempt and all too often one sees plaice described as 'the least interesting in flavour of the flat fish' and 'economically but not gastronomically the most important flat fish'. I rather think that the fault lies not with the fish but with the cook for while the flesh is white, moist and delicately flavoured it is also extremely fragile. Plaice is usually cooked with the skin on but even so care must be taken not to overcook it.

Small plaice can be cooked whole but larger ones are

nearly always filleted. There is no difference in quality between the dark and white fillets and it is usual for fish-mongers to give their customers equal numbers of each. They can be coated in batter or egg and breadcrumbs and deep-fried or grilled, baked, steamed or poached.

Plaice can be treated as if they were Dover sole provided that they are not cooked a minute longer than necessary and are not kept waiting. The classic sauces served with plaice are hollandaise or tartare but I prefer not to mask its delicate flavour or texture with anything quite so heavy and I like to serve it simply with lemon juice and perhaps a knob of butter.

Although available all year round plaice is at its best from May through to January.

STEAMED FISH CHINESE STYLE

4 plaice fillets
225g/8 oz button mushrooms, sliced
2 shallots, finely chopped
2 tsps arrowroot
2 tbsps shoyu **soy sauce**
4 tbsps sesame oil
1 tbsp dry white wine

Brush four pieces of foil with oil, lay a fillet on top of each and cover with the mushrooms and shallots. Blend the remaining ingredients together and pour over the fish. Fold the foil *en papillote* to form a loose sealed parcel, place in the bottom of a large steamer and cover. Bring a large pan of water to the boil, stand the steamer on top and cook for 10–15 minutes. Serve immediately with brown rice.

LEMON PLAICE WITH VEGETABLES

100g/4 oz French beans, trimmed
2–3 courgettes, sliced
100g/4 oz button mushrooms, sliced
450–675g/1–1½ lbs plaice fillets
1 tbsp finely chopped fresh thyme
juice of 1 lemon
freshly ground black pepper

Put the French beans in a steamer, cover and stand over a pan of boiling water. Cook for 4–5 minutes before adding the courgettes and mushrooms. Quickly cut the plaice into strips measuring 3.75 × 1.25 cm/ 1½ × ½ inch and lay on top of the vegetables. Add the thyme, cover and steam for 2–3 minutes more until the vegetables and fish are tender. Carefully turn out onto a warm serving dish and sprinkle the lemon juice over the top. Season with black pepper. Serve immediately with new potatoes or brown rice.

PLAICE À LA NORMANDE

**900g/2 lbs mussels
150ml/¼ pint dry white wine
1 sprig of fresh parsley
1 sprig of fresh thyme
1 slice of onion
6 black peppercorns
675g/1½ lbs plaice fillets
100g/4 oz button mushrooms, sliced
juice of ½ lemon
seasoning
150ml/¼ pint fish stock/water (p. 41)**

Clean the mussels as described on page 27. Put into a large pan with the wine, parsley, thyme, onion and peppercorns. Cover and place over a moderate heat. Cook for 2–3 minutes, shaking the pan frequently until most of the mussels have opened. Discard any that do not. Strain the cooking stock through a piece of damp muslin and keep aside until needed. Remove the mussels from the open shells and reserve.

Arrange the plaice fillets in the bottom of a large pan and scatter the mushrooms on top. Add the lemon juice and season to taste. Now pour over the reserved mussel stock and sufficient fish stock or water to barely cover the plaice. Cover with a lid and bring to a slow boil. Reduce the heat and poach for 3–4 minutes. Add the mussels and continue to cook for a further 2–3 minutes until the fish is tender.

PRAWNS

These days most of the prawns on sale are pre-boiled and just need heating up in a hot oven or in a sauce; larger ones can be brushed with oil and grilled. Only the fleshy tails of prawns are eaten, the rest being discarded or used to make stocks and sauces. To peel a prawn, first pull away the head and then unwrap the armoured shell from the body and legs – it should come away in one piece. In all but the smallest prawns the dark, thread-like gut running along the back needs to be removed also.

Fresh prawns are far better than frozen ones and those caught in cold waters are reputed to have a much finer flavour than warm-water creatures. Prawns have an affinity with rice and eggs but they can be used to add interest and flavour to a wide range of dishes, from soups to sandwiches.

SAFFRON SEAFOOD SALAD

**225g/8 oz long grain brown rice
a good pinch of saffron strands
575ml/1 pint water
75g/3 oz garden peas, cooked
75g/3 oz peeled prawns
75g/3 oz shelled mussels
½ red pepper, chopped
juice of 1 lemon
3 tbsps olive oil
a dash of white wine vinegar
seasoning**

Put the rice and saffron into a heavy pan. Pour over the water and bring to the boil. Cover and simmer gently, without stirring, for 35–40 minutes until all the water has been absorbed and the rice is dry and tender. Add the

peas, prawns, mussels and red pepper. Blend the lemon juice and oil together and add a dash of wine vinegar to taste. Pour over the hot rice and toss well. Season to taste. Leave to cool.

PRAWN CURRY

**1–2 tbsps groundnut oil
1 large onion, chopped
1 stick of celery, finely chopped
2 cloves of garlic, peeled and crushed
2 tsps ground coriander
1 tsp turmeric
1 tsp ground cumin
125ml/4 fl. oz water
125ml/4 fl. oz natural yoghurt
675g/1½ lbs peeled prawns
juice of ½–1 lemon
2 tbsps chopped fresh coriander**

Heat the oil in a large pan, add the onion and celery and sauté for 5–7 minutes until they soften and turn golden brown. Add the garlic and the spices and cook for 2–3 minutes more, stirring frequently. Pour over the water and bring to the boil. Cook gently for 3 minutes before stirring in the yoghurt and the prawns. Cover and simmer for 8–10 minutes until the prawns are heated through. Season to taste with lemon juice. Sprinkle with fresh coriander before serving.

Facing page 112: Kulebiaca (pages 120–121); photograph courtesy of the Scottish Salmon Information Service.
Left: Basic ingredients for Kedgeree (page 138); photograph courtesy of the Milk Marketing Board.

MALAYSIAN FRIED VEGETABLES WITH PRAWNS

**2 tbsps groundnut oil
1 onion, chopped
1 clove of garlic, peeled and crushed
1 green chilli, finely chopped
2.5 cm/1 inch fresh root ginger, peeled and grated
225g/8 oz French beans, sliced
1 red pepper, sliced
4 courgettes, sliced
2 tbsps ground almonds
1 tbsp** shoyu **soy sauce
225g/8 oz peeled prawns**

Heat the oil in a wok. Add the onion, garlic, chilli and ginger and stir-fry for several minutes. Meanwhile blanch the French beans for 2–3 minutes and then drain. Toss them into the wok with the red pepper and courgettes. Stir-fry for several minutes before adding the ground almonds and soy sauce. Carefully mix in the prawns and continue to cook, stirring occasionally, until the vegetables are tender and the prawns are heated through.

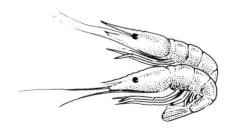

CHINESE RICE WITH PRAWNS AND EGG FOO YUNG

225g/8 oz long grain brown rice
a scant 575ml/1 pint water
2 tbsps groundnut oil
1 onion, finely chopped
100g/4 oz mushrooms, sliced
100g/4 oz garden peas, cooked
100g/4 oz peeled prawns
seasoning
2 large eggs
1–2 tsps shoyu **soy sauce**
15g/½ oz butter

Put the rice in a heavy pan and pour over the water. Cover and bring to the boil. Simmer for 35–40 minutes, without stirring, until all the water has been absorbed and the rice is dry and tender. Remove from the heat but keep covered until needed.

Heat the oil in a large frying pan or wok. Add the onion and stir-fry for several minutes until it begins to soften. Then toss in the mushrooms, peas and prawns and cook for a further minutes. Add the rice and cook until heated through, stirring frequently. Season to taste.

Meanwhile beat the eggs and soy sauce together. Melt the butter in a small frying pan and when foaming pour in the egg mixture. Cook until the underneath is firm and patterned golden brown. Flip over and cook the other side too. Cut into strips and carefully stir into the rice mixture. Serve.

MEDITERRANEAN RICE

A rather extravagant dish combining the delicious flavours, colours and textures of prawns, pine kernels, rice and Mediterranean vegetables topped with a crusty layer of golden, bubbling cheese. It is ideal for special occasions as it can be made in advance and heated through in the oven when needed.

275g/10 oz long grain brown rice
a scant 725ml/1¼ pints water
2 tbsps olive oil
1 onion, sliced
1 clove of garlic, peeled and crushed
1 green pepper, chopped
3 tomatoes, diced
100g/4 oz frozen peas
100g/4 oz peeled prawns
50g/2 oz pine kernels
freshly ground black pepper
75g/3 oz Gruyère cheese, grated
25g/1 oz Parmesan cheese, grated

Put the rice and the water in a heavy pan, cover and bring to the boil. Simmer, without stirring, for 35–40 minutes until all the water has been absorbed and the rice is dry and tender. Remove from the heat but leave covered until needed.

Heat the oil in a frying pan, add the onion and garlic and sauté until soft and golden. Then add the green pepper, the tomatoes and peas. Cook gently for a further 5–8 minutes, stirring frequently, until the vegetables begin to soften. Add the prawns and pine kernels and cook for a few minutes more. There will be about 3–4 tablespoons of stock in the bottom of the pan.

Carefully mix the vegetable and fish mixture with the

hot cooked rice and season to taste with black pepper. Spoon into a lightly oiled, shallow ovenproof dish and sprinkle the grated Gruyère and Parmesan over the top. Put in a hot oven or under a hot grill until the cheese is bubbling. Serve with a tossed salad.

RAY, *see* Skate

RED MULLET

The name red mullet refers to two very similar species of fish found principally in the Mediterranean, although other members of the same family can be found in Caribbean waters and the Indo-Pacific Sea. Perhaps because of their warm, rich colouring I have always associated them with blue seas and sunny climates and was surprised to read in *Kettner's Book of the Table* (written in the late nineteenth century by E.S. Dallas) that red mullet could be bought in Britain throughout the year, although he does add that they were at their best from midsummer to Christmas. Apparently prize catches were to be found off the coast near Weymouth, and it is reported that would-be gourmets used to summer there with the intention of savouring the mullet.

The Romans too are said to have had a passion for this fish, so much so that at one time Emperor Tiberius had to pay a sum equivalent to £200 for just one fish. Not only did the Romans enjoy the culinary charms of the red mullet but they also kept them in tanks, very much as we keep tropical fish today, admiring their plump attractive bodies which are a dusky pink on the back, the sides rippled with a golden flash, and the belly fading to a delicate silvery hue.

The red mullet can be confused with the red gurnard, both having similar colouring. However, they have very little else in common. The gurnard has a much larger, bonier head and is without the two barbels which protrude beneath the red mullet's chin. These barbels are characteristic of all the members of the red mullet family which have been nicknamed goatfish in many parts of the world. The most important difference between the gurnard and the mullet is the quality of the meat. In this respect the red mullet is a clear winner.

The red mullet is also known as the 'sea woodcock' for like the game bird of that name its flavour is said to improve if cooked and served without first being gutted. I have even read of one cook who suggested 'hanging' the fish for 24 hours before cooking it. I will be the first to admit to having neither the confidence nor the stomach to prepare red mullet in this manner. Far too many of today's fish are caught and deep frozen in the Mediterranean and there is always some doubt in my mind as to their freshness. Who can tell how long they have been sitting around while thawing out?

In fact current opinion seems in general to be erring on the side of caution and most modern cookery books recommend removing the guts of all but the smallest fish. Ideally the fish should be cleaned through the gills, keeping its round chubby body intact. However, I generally clean it from a small incision in the belly, for I can imagine, all too vividly, the commotion that would ensue if one of my family found a piece of entrail, no matter how small, lurking inside their fish. I am afraid that they would not be mollified in the slightest by the knowledge that some of the world's leading gourmets regard such things, in particular the red mullet's liver, as a great delicacy.

It is generally agreed that the liver should be left in the red mullet or incorporated into a sauce or pâté. However, it is curious how few writers give instructions as to how best this is achieved. In this repect my thanks go to George Lassalle who gives the following advice in *The Adventurous Fish Cook* (Papermac, 1982): '[the liver] can be located near the thickest complex of blood vessels [the heart] of the fish, partially surrounding the intestines at the front end of the fish.'

If the idea of poking around inside a red mullet does not appeal, please don't let this small detail stop you from experimenting with the fish. Perhaps your fishmonger could gut it for you, retaining or removing the liver according to your wishes. I always enjoy red mullet, with or without its liver. The meat is white and firm and has a distinctive and fairly strong taste.

It goes particularly well with Mediterranean flavours such as fennel, tomatoes, garlic, saffron, rosemary and basil.

A single red mullet can weigh up to 1.5–2 kg/3–4½ lbs but they are generally caught weighing between 175–225g/6–8 oz, an ideal size for one person. They are usually sold whole and need to be gutted, scaled and trimmed before being cooked. Good ways of cooking red mullet are grilling and baking. They also make good pâtés and terrines although care must be taken to remove all the small bones. Perhaps the best way to cook red mullet is *en papillote*. Here is Kettner's recipe which tastes as good today as it must have done over a hundred years ago although you may prefer to wrap the mullet inside a loose but secure foil parcel as described on page 37.

RED MULLET EN PAPILLOTE

'Make a paper cradle for each fish, oiling it and baking it for a few minutes in order to harden it. Sprinkle the cradle with salt and pepper, and lay on it a piece of best fresh butter. On this couch deposit the red mullet, and put a piece of fresh butter over him. Arrange the paper cases in a flat stewpan, or even a baking tray, and put them into the oven for twenty or thirty minutes [at a moderate temperature]. At the end of this time the red mullet, bedewed with lemon juice, will be as pleasant to taste as [it is] lovely to look at'.

RED MULLET NIÇOISE STYLE

1–2 tbsps olive oil
4 red mullet, scaled, trimmed and cleaned
225g/8 oz tomatoes, chopped
2 shallots, finely chopped
6–8 black olives, stoned and chopped
freshly ground black pepper
1 tbsp finely chopped fresh parsley
75–150ml/3–5 fl. oz dry white wine

Brush a shallow ovenproof dish with olive oil. Arrange the fish in the bottom and sprinkle with the tomatoes, shallots and olives. Season with black pepper and parsley. Pour over the wine and bake in a preheated oven, gas mark 5 (190° C/375° F), for 20–25 minutes.

RED MULLET WITH FENNEL AND TOMATO

Red mullet with fennel is enjoying something of a revival at the present time. To be authentic the fish must be brushed with oil or butter and grilled on a bed of dried fennel stalks. When cooked a ladleful of flaming brandy is poured over the mullet. The fennel twigs give off a wonderfully woody and aniseedy smell which permeates the fish and whets the appetite of all those in the vicinity.

Unfortunately woody fennel stalks are not readily available here in Britain. Instead I use the bulbous Florence fennel. The dish is not quite so dramatic, perhaps, but it tastes very good!

1–2 tbsps olive oil
1 Florence fennel bulb, thinly sliced
225g/8 oz tomatoes, diced
1 lemon
several sprigs of fresh parsley
freshly ground black pepper
1 tsp tomato purée (optional)
4 red mullet, weighing 175–225g/6–8 oz each

Heat 1 tablespoon of oil in a pan, add the fennel and sauté for 3–4 minutes until lightly coloured. Add the tomatoes, the grated rind and juice of half the lemon and 1 tablespoon finely chopped parsley. Cover and cook gently, stirring occasionally, for 8–10 minutes. Season to taste and add the tomato purée if using it. Spoon the mixture into an ovenproof dish.

Scale and clean the fish, leaving the heads in situ. Wash carefully and pat dry. Make two to three cuts in both sides of each fish. Put a small sprig of parsley in each of the cuts running down one side of the fish and then arrange the mullet, parsley down, on top of the fennel mixture. Brush with olive oil. Cut the remaining half lemon into thin slices and then in half again. Push a piece of lemon into each of the cuts on the exposed sides of the fish and cover the dish with foil. Bake in a preheated oven, gas mark 4 (180° C/350° F), for 25–30 minutes.

GRILLED MULLET WITH YOGHURT

4 red mullet, scaled, trimmed and cleaned
olive oil

FOR THE SAUCE
150ml/¼ pint natural yoghurt
2 egg yolks
1 tsp lemon juice
freshly ground black pepper
2 tbsps finely chopped fresh herbs
(mixed parsley, chervil, tarragon)

Make two to three deep gashes in the sides of each fish. Brush with oil and place under a hot grill. Cook for 5–7 minutes on both sides.

Meanwhile beat the yoghurt, egg yolks and lemon juice together. Place in a small bowl over a pan of simmering water. Cook gently, stirring all the time, until the sauce begins to thicken. It will take between 10–15 minutes. Season to taste with black pepper and stir in the herbs. Serve with the fish.

GRILLED RED MULLET

Scale and clean the fish. Rinse well and pat dry. Make several diagonal cuts on both sides of the fish and season with a little freshly ground black pepper. Brush with olive oil and place under a hot grill. After a minute or two reduce the heat and cook for 5–7 minutes on both sides. Serve with melted butter mixed with a little finely chopped shallot and lemon juice.

RED MULLET WITH MUSHROOMS

4 red mullet
275ml/½ pint dry white wine
100g/4 oz button mushrooms, sliced
seasoning
2 tbsps soft wholewheat breadcrumbs
25g/1 oz butter

Clean, scale and trim the fish. Place in a buttered oven-proof dish. Pour over the wine and cover with mushrooms. Season to taste. Bake in a preheated oven, gas mark 4 (180° C/350° F), for 20–25 minutes, basting frequently. Sprinkle with breadcrumbs and dot with butter. Turn up the oven temperature to gas mark 7 (220° C/425°F) and put back on the top shelf for 10 minutes or under a hot grill until the breadcrumbs begin to brown.

RED MULLET ORIENTAL

I first came across this recipe while reading *Alice Toklas's Cookbook* (Brilliance Books, 1983), and thought at the time that it sounded very good. I made a mental note to try it one day but, of course, it completely slipped my mind until I saw it again, several months later, in Jane Grigson's *Fish Cookery* (Wine and Food Society, 1973).

4 red mullet
675g/1½ lbs tomatoes, chopped
150ml/¼ pint dry white wine
a good pinch of saffron strands
1 tsp mixed dried herbs
1 bay leaf
a pinch of ground coriander
1 clove of garlic, peeled and crushed
seasoning

Scale, trim and clean the fish. Place in a shallow, oiled ovenproof dish. Put all the remaining ingredients together in a pan and bring to the boil. Cover and cook gently until the tomatoes are very soft and the sauce has thickened. Season to taste. Pour over the fish and bake in a preheated oven, gas mark 7 (220° C/425° F), for 10–12 minutes. Leave to get cold and serve chilled.

S

SALMON

Not so long ago salmon were abundant in our rivers and estuaries, so much so that they could be bought for next to nothing. Instead of appearing on the tables of the rich they were one of the staple foods eaten by the poor, and many young apprentices complained bitterly if they were given salmon more than twice a week. Times have changed. Wild salmon are now so scarce that they fetch very high prices and are unlikely to be served up by the typical landlady once a year let alone twice a week.

The salmon, with its pink-coloured flesh and rich distinctive flavour, has been described as 'the king of the fish'. While it is not one of my favourites I do think that a whole poached salmon, arranged on a silver tray and garnished with slivers of cucumber and lemon and sprigs of parsley is one of the finest dishes to serve at a large gathering or function. The salmon's silvery skin, shimmering with the colours of the rainbow, looks magnificent and needs little in the way of embellishment. It certainly does not need covering in royal blue aspic as I have seen at one reception.

Salmon are unusual fish for they spend half their lives in fresh water and the other half in the sea. British salmon are spawned in the upper reaches of many of our rivers where they stay for up to three years before swimming to the cold waters off Greenland. Three to four years later they return to the rivers to spawn. Once they have reached maturity salmon are only able to feed in sea water and so they arrive off our coasts plump, firm, well nourished and physically prepared for the lean days ahead. This is the best time to catch them for after they have spawned they are mere shadows of their former selves and are often so exhausted that they can be seen drifting down river and out to sea tail first. Few survive this journey and those that live are not fit to eat.

The number of salmon being caught in our rivers is falling alarmingly. Pollution is partly to blame but it is also due to the large number of trawlers used to catch the fish in the deep waters off Greenland. As a result fewer fish are given the chance to return to their native rivers to spawn. Fortunately for salmon lovers salmon farms have been fairly successful and although gourmets claim that farmed salmon are not as tasty as wild ones they still make splendid eating and certainly help to keep supplies up and prices down.

Scotch salmon is considered to be the finest in the world, and as with most fish the fresher the better. Middle cuts are generally regarded to be the best as salmon, particularly large ones, have a tendency to dryness. Fresh salmon are available from February to August and are especially good in the spring.

One of the nicest ways, and some would say the only way, to prepare a whole salmon is to poach it in court-bouillon. The traditional accompaniments are hollandaise sauce, *beurre blanc* or melted butter, new potatoes and green peas. As few people today possess a fish kettle a good alternative to poaching the fish is to cook it *en papillote*. Small whole fish (1–1.25 kg/2–2¾ lbs) and steaks can be baked in this way. The fish is sealed inside buttered foil, perhaps with a knob of butter, a tablespoon or two of dry white wine, a sprig of two of fresh herbs and some seasoning. Cooked in a preheated oven, gas mark 4 (180° C/350° F) it will be ready in 40–50 minutes. Remember when cooking salmon that thickness is as important as weight. To test the fish open the parcel carefully so as not to spill any of the cooking juices and use a sharp knife or skewer to see if the fish comes cleanly from the bone. If the salmon is to be eaten cold leave wrapped up until needed.

Last but not least, I must mention smoked salmon which, to my mind, is far superior to fresh salmon. It is hard to imagine a finer meal than a few tender, moist slices of smoked salmon eaten with brown bread and butter and wedges of lemon. Always buy it from a whole fish and make sure that each slice is wafer thin (see Smoked Fish section as well).

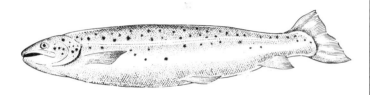

OVEN-BAKED SALMON

If you don't possess a fish kettle and can't hire one, place the cleaned salmon on a large sheet of buttered foil and season well. Fold the foil *en papillote* to form a loose parcel and bake in a preheated oven, gas mark 2 (150° C/300° F) for 1 hour for a fish weighing up to 2.25kg/5 lbs or 12 minutes per 450g/1 lb for any over that weight. Any whole fish can be cooked this way.

KULEBIAKA

Also known as *coulibiac*, this impressive fish pie originates from Russia. It has been described as 'a superb, complicated invention consisting of layers of tender strips of boneless salmon covered with a sauce velouté and matchlessly seasoned with dill and mushrooms encased in a fresh yeasty brioche pastry' (*Classic French Cooking*, Time Life Books, 1978). Melted butter and, in some cases, cream were poured into the pastry case before the hot pie was rushed to the table.

An impressive description to be sure, but don't be misled. Kulebiaka is, first and foremost, a family dish, and like so many East European dishes traditionally was made from hearty, robust ingredients designed to keep out the cold rather than to impress guests.

200g/7 oz strong bread flour
¼ tsp cream of tartar
butter
6–7 tbsps cold water
a little milk to glaze

FOR THE FILLING
350g/12 oz salmon steaks
approx. 275ml/½ pint water
1 bay leaf
½ carrot, sliced
fresh parsley
1 tbsp sunflower oil
1 onion, chopped
75g/3 oz buckwheat or long grain rice
100g/4 oz button mushrooms, sliced
juice of ½ lemon
seasoning
2 hard-boiled eggs, sliced

To make the pastry, mix the flour and cream of tartar together in a bowl. Add 25g/1 oz butter and rub in with the fingertips. Add the water and, with a fork, mix to form a soft dough. Turn onto a floured board and knead lightly until smooth and pliant. Wrap in polythene and put in a cool place to rest for 30 minutes.

Sprinkle 100–120g/4 oz butter with a little extra flour and, with a rolling pin, beat out to form a neat oblong 1.25 cm/½ inch thick. Roll out the rested dough to an oblong a little larger than the butter shape and long enough for the two ends of the dough to fold over the butter (overlapping slightly). Place the butter in the centre and fold the pastry over to completely cover it. Press the edges together to seal. Give the dough a half turn to bring the open ends to the top and bottom. With the rolling pin press the dough gently, from the centre to the top and bottom, and then quickly and lightly roll out the dough to an oblong three times as long as it is wide. (Don't roll out too thinly or the layers of dough and butter will merge.) Mark the pastry into thirds (don't cut through the dough) and fold the bottom third over the centre and the top third down over both. Seal the edges and give the pastry a half turn. Repeat the rolling and folding once more then wrap in polythene and chill for 30 minutes.

After two further turns, rolls and folds the pastry must rest again. Turn, roll and fold twice more. The pastry is now ready for use.

To make the filling, put the salmon in a small pan and barely cover with water. Add the bay leaf, carrot and a sprig of parsley and bring to a very slow boil. Reduce the heat until the water is hardly moving, cover, and poach for 5–8 minutes. When tender, lift from the pan with a slotted spoon and keep aside. Strain and reserve the stock.

Heat the oil in a pan, add the onion and sauté for 5–7 minutes until soft and golden. Meanwhile place the buckwheat in another pan and dry-fry, without adding any oil or water, but stirring frequently, until the grains begin to darken. Tip from the pan as soon as they begin to colour so that they do not burn. Stir the buckwheat into the sautéed onions and pour over 225ml/8 fl. oz cooking stock (from the salmon). Bring to the boil, cover and simmer for 10–15 minutes until all the liquid has been absorbed and the buckwheat is dry and tender. If using rice, simply simmer it in plenty of water until tender, drain well and add to the onions.

Melt a knob of butter in a pan, add the mushrooms and sauté for 3–4 minutes. Remove the skin and bones from the salmon and break into flakes. Gently stir into the mushrooms. Pour over the lemon juice, cover and cook for several minutes more, stirring frequently to prevent the salmon sticking to the pan. Add the buckwheat and 2 tablespoons finely chopped parsley and season to taste. The mixture should be fairly dry. Leave to cool.

Cut the pastry in half and roll out to form two rectangles, approximately 50 × 20 cm/10 × 8 inches, one slightly larger than the other. Place the larger pastry rectangle on a baking tray and spoon over the filling, leaving a 2.5-cm/1-inch margin around the edge. Arrange the hard-boiled eggs on top and cover with the remaining pastry. Dampen the edges, press together to seal and trim. Make two cuts in the top of the pastry to let the steam escape, and brush with milk. Bake in a preheated oven, gas mark 7 (220°C/425°F), for 30–35 minutes. Cover with greaseproof paper if the pastry top browns too quickly.

Kulebiaca is delicious served hot or cold with soured cream.

FRESH SALMON QUICHE

A useful way of using up a small amount of leftover cooked salmon. The quiche is light, delicately coloured and beautifully flavoured, and makes an ideal lunch or supper dish in the late spring and summer.

175g/6 oz wholewheat flour
75g/3 oz butter, diced
6 tsps cold water

FOR THE FILLING
175g/6 oz cooked salmon
1 tbsp finely chopped fresh parsley
3 eggs
150ml/¼ pint natural yoghurt
freshly ground black pepper
1 tbsp grated Parmesan cheese

For the pastry, put the flour in a bowl and rub in the butter until the mixture resembles breadcrumbs. Stir in the water and mix to form a pastry dough. Turn out onto a lightly floured work surface, roll out and line a 20 cm/8 inch flan ring. Prick the pastry base with a fork and blind-bake in a preheated oven, gas mark 6 (200° C/400° F), for 10 minutes.

For the filling, remove the skin and any bones from the fish and break into flakes. Put the fish flakes in the bottom of the blind-baked pastry case and sprinkle the parsley on top. Beat the eggs and yoghurt together and season with black pepper. Pour over the fish and top with Parmesan cheese. Return to the oven and bake for 25 minutes. Serve warm or cold.

FRESH SALMON PASTE

Salmon paste is usually eaten in small amounts, not for the obvious reasons of cost but because it is very rich and filling. I sometimes make it a little lighter in texture, taste and calories by replacing some of the butter with low-fat cream cheese, in which case you also need to omit the 3–4 tablespoons of reduced court-bouillon from the mixture, otherwise the paste becomes too soft.

225g/8 oz salmon steaks
approx. 275ml/½ pint court-bouillon (p. 40)
100g/4 oz soft butter
1 tbsp finely chopped fresh parsley
1 clove of garlic, peeled and crushed
a pinch of cayenne pepper
grated rind and juice of 1 lemon
seasoning

Put the fish into a pan and barely cover with court-bouillon. Bring to a very slow boil, reduce the heat and when the surface is barely moving cover and poach for 5–8 minutes. When tender lift from the pan with a slotted spoon and leave to cool. Bring the court-bouillon to a fast boil and cook, uncovered, until reduced to about 3–4 tablespoons.

Put the butter into a small bowl and cream until very soft and smooth. When the fish is cool remove the skin and bones and pass the flakes through a vegetable mouli or food processor. Add the other ingredients, including the reduced court-bouillon, and mix together well. Adjust the seasoning to taste, and spoon into an attractive pot. Cover and leave in a cool place to firm up. Serve with thin slices of buttered wholewheat bread and slivers of cucumber.

SALMON TROUT

This fish should, strictly speaking, be known as the sea trout but most people, including fishmongers, call it salmon trout for it combines the very best of both these fish. It has been described as 'the perfect fish' and, as far as freshwater fish go, has a reputation second to none.

Like the salmon, salmon trout spends most of its life in the sea, living off small crustaceans which give its flesh the characteristic orangey-pink colouring, and it only enters freshwater rivers to spawn. The similarity in appearance and habitat between the salmon, salmon trout and trout has caused much confusion over the centuries as can be seen from this passage, written in the fourth century by a Latin scholar living in Bordeaux.

'And thou, who, between two species, is of neither,
Not yet a salmon, nor not still a trout
Ambiguously placed between the pair,
O salmon trout, taken between two ages.'

The three fish are so similar that it would not have seemed outrageous to suggest that the trout was the offspring, the salmon trout the adolescent of the family and the salmon the mature adult. By the nineteenth century this idea had been dropped in favour of a more reasoned and scientific explanation. To say that anglers and gourmets recognised the salmon trout as a separate species of fish is not strictly correct for they saw it more as a 'freak', one of nature's little mistakes, which turned up once in a while as a result of a trout inadvertently mating with a salmon. The record has since been put straight and although the salmon trout is accepted as being a close relative of both the trout and the salmon it is nevertheless regarded as a species in its own right (*salmo trutta*).

Small salmon trout can be treated like trout and are perhaps best when grilled and served with melted butter. Larger fish, weighing anything from 675g–2kg/1½–4½

lbs, are either sold whole or as steaks and seem to have more in common with the salmon. Like the salmon they make an excellent luncheon or dinner dish for family gatherings or more formal occasions, and can be served hot or cold. They can be poached, grilled or baked but by far the best way of cooking them is *en papillote* with a sprig of thyme and knob of butter. Accompaniments should be kept light in flavour and texture so that they do not drown the fish itself.

Although salmon trout is less rich and heavy than salmon, it is still fairly filling and 175–225-g/6–8-oz portions are sufficient for most people. The fish is at its best in late spring and early summer by which time it has recovered its weight and condition after winter spawning.

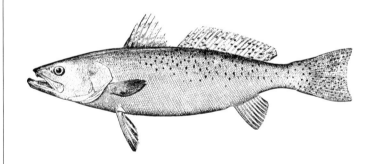

SALMON TROUT EN PAPILLOTE WITH BEURRE BLANC SAUCE

Cooking the steaks *en papillote* seals in their natural juices and guards against the tendency to dryness while the final addition of the *beurre blanc* sauce adds a hint of piquancy which complements the richness of the fish perfectly.

15g/½ oz butter, melted
4 salmon trout steaks
freshly ground black pepper
4 sprigs of fresh parsley
4 slices of lemon
Beurre Blanc sauce (p. 49)

Cut four sheets of greaseproof paper, so that each is large enough to wrap around one of the steaks. Brush with melted butter and then place one piece of fish in the centre of each sheet. Season with black pepper and lay a sprig of parsley and a slice of lemon on top. Fold the paper over the fish, tucking the ends underneath, to form a secure parcel. Place on a baking tray and bake in a preheated oven, gas mark 6 (200° C/400° F), for 15–20 minutes until tender.

Meanwhile prepare the sauce as described on page 49.

When the salmon trout is cooked unwrap each parcel, taking care not to spill the cooking juices. Lay the fish on warm plates and pour over the cooking juices. Put the sauce in a small bowl or sauce boat and serve with the fish. Lightly boiled new potatoes and mange tout peas or green beans are excellent accompaniments to this dish.

COLD SALMON TROUT WITH SAUCE MALTAISE

Elizabeth David gives the following advice in her excellent book, *Summer Cooking* (Penguin Books, 1965): 'If you have no fish-kettle, cook it in a baking tin in the oven, in a little salted water, allowing about 15 minutes to the pound in a medium to slow oven. If it is to be served cold, let it cool before lifting it out and it will be easier to handle. Serve it on a long dish with a ring of finely sliced and lightly salted cucumber all round it, and, better than hollandaise, a sauce maltaise.' The Maltaise sauce on page 51, made from hollandaise with the juice of a blood orange instead of lemon is particularly delicious.

SALMON TROUT POACHED IN WHITE WINE

4 salmon trout steaks, weighing approx.
175g/6 oz each
freshly ground black pepper
25g/1 oz butter
150ml/¼ pint dry white wine

Season the fish with black pepper. Melt the butter in a heavy frying pan and add the fish. Cook quickly on each side before pouring the wine over the top. When the wine has begun to bubble reduce the heat, cover and poach the fish for 5–8 minutes until tender. Carefully remove the fish and place on a serving dish. Cover and keep warm. Bring the stock to the boil and cook fiercely until much reduced. Pour over the fish before serving.

SALMON TROUT WITH CUCUMBER SAUCE

4 salmon steaks
approx. 425ml/¾ pint court-bouillon (p. 40)
Cucumber Sauce (p. 47)

Put the fish in a pan and barely cover with court-bouillon. Bring to a very slow boil, reduce the heat, cover and poach for 5–8 minutes until tender.

Meanwhile make the sauce as described on page 47. Once smooth, return the sauce to the pan and heat through, stirring frequently. Add a little of the court-bouillon if it is too thick. Season to taste. Serve with the hot poached fish.

SALT COD

Dried salt cod was once an important food throughout Europe and North America satisfying the demand in Roman Catholic areas for fish on Fridays and Lenten days. It was cheap and easy to transport, but gradually its popularity has waned and now it is only eaten in any quantity in the poorer regions of the Mediterranean and in West Indian communities. It is sold in solid, greyish blocks and needs to be soaked to restore its original colour, plumpness and tenderness and, of course, to remove the salt used to preserve it.

To reconstitute salt cod, cover with cold water and soak for at least 24 hours, changing the water every 4–6 hours. Drain well. The fish is now ready to be cooked. A simple method of cooking salt cod is to chop it up and put it into a clean pan. Barely cover with water and poach for 15–20 minutes until tender. It is particularly good served with *aïoli*, a garlic mayonnaise from Provence (p. 52) or cooked with tomatoes and chillies as in the following recipe.. Salt cod can also be used to make hearty stews and is often cooked with potatoes, beans, chick peas and onion.

CARIBBEAN SALT COD

225g/8 oz salt cod
50g/2 oz salt pork, finely chopped
1 onion, chopped
1 small green pepper, chopped
1 small red chilli, finely chopped
2 tomatoes, chopped
a pinch of dried thyme
freshly ground black pepper
3 slices of lean plain bacon
1–2 tbsps finely chopped fresh parsley

Soak the salt cod for 24 hours, changing the water regularly. Drain well and chop into pieces. Put into a pan and barely cover with water. Poach for 15 minutes. Lift from the pan and when cool enough to handle remove the skin and bones and flake.

Meanwhile fry the salt pork until crisp and brown. Remove from the pan and keep aside. Put the onion, green pepper and chilli into the pan and sauté until soft. Add the tomatoes and cook gently until they too begin to soften. Put the salt cod and salt pork into the pan and heat through. Season with thyme and black pepper. Grill the bacon and lay on top of the dish. Sprinkle with parsley before taking to the table.

SARDINES

I have never had the pleasure of eating fresh sardines (fresh as opposed to frozen), but I am told that they taste wonderful, particularly when grilled over charcoal and eaten with a glass of red wine on a terrace overlooking the sea. Sardines spend most of their lives basking in the warm Mediterranean, venturing north as far as the Bay of Biscay in the summer when things get a little too hot at home. They take their name from the island of Sardinia around whose coastline they thrive – or at least they did until fishing became a big and sophisticated business.

Sardines are poor travellers and begin to deteriorate almost as soon as they have left the water. Although we are unlikely to see fresh sardines in our shops it is not unusual to see small boxes, tightly packed, with frozen silvery sardines. Enthusiasts, I am sure, would be able to tell them from the genuine article but they still taste very good and are much nicer than canned varieties.

I was surprised to learn that canned sardines are collectors' items and that before the war Oscar Wilde's son founded a vintage sardine club where members could discuss the serious business of laying down cans of sardines. Apparently canned sardines actually improve with age and were kept for up to five years before being savoured as if they were a great wine. Manufacturers too used to keep their sardines in oil-filled vats for at least a year before permitting them to be canned. Alas in these days of financial hardships and rising business costs most sardines are whipped into their cans before they have had time to say Jack Robinson. To make matters even worse most companies have stopped using olive oil, replacing it with cheaper vegetable oils; some even use tomato sauce!

Canned sardines have many uses. Serve them as hors d'oeuvres, hot on buttered toast, in pastes and pâtés, stuffed inside baked potatoes, in omelettes, with scrambled eggs and in fish cakes. Fresh ones, however, are delicious simply grilled or fried and served with brown bread and lemon juice. Allow four to six sardines per person, depending on size.

FRESH SARDINE FILLING FOR OMELETTES

6–7 fresh or frozen sardines (thaw out if necessary)
juice of 1 lemon
2 tbsps finely chopped fresh parsley
seasoning

Cut off and discard the heads and tails of the sardines. Split them open along the belly and clean well. Spread the fish open and lay them, skin uppermost, on a chopping board or work surface. Press down gently but firmly on the backbone. Turn over and carefully remove the bones.

Heat a heavy frying pan and add the sardines. Dry-fry for several minutes on each side until cooked through. Place in a bowl and mash with a fork. Add the lemon juice and parsley, and season to taste. Keep warm while cooking the omelettes. Spoon some the filling into the centre of each omelette before taking to the table.

COURGETTES STUFFED WITH SARDINES

This recipe is excellent made with fresh or canned sardines. If using fresh ones, first remove the bones and dry-fry as described in the recipe above.

4 medium to large courgettes

FOR THE FILLING
4–6 tbsps cooked brown rice
4–6 sardines, chopped
25g/1 oz pine kernels
25g/1 oz sultanas
1–2 tbsps chopped fresh parsley
1–2 tsps tomato purée
a good pinch of ground cinnamon
seasoning

FOR THE TOPPING
275ml/½ pint natural yoghurt
2 egg yolks

Trim the courgettes and cut in half lengthways. Scoop out the spongy centre from each half, chop and place in a mixing bowl. Stir in the filling ingredients and season to taste. Meanwhile put the hollowed-out courgettes in a steamer and steam for 5 minutes until they begin to soften. Spoon the filling into the courgettes and arrange in a shallow ovenproof dish. Beat the yoghurt and egg yolks together and pour over the courgettes. Bake in a pre-heated oven, gas mark 6 (200° C/400° F), for 20 minutes until heated through.

TOSSED SARDINES

2 tsps olive oil
3 cloves of garlic, peeled and crushed
1 tbsp finely chopped fresh parsley
juice of ½ lemon
2 tbsps dry white wine
450g/1 lb sardines, cleaned and boned

Place all the ingredients in a large heavy pan. Stir-fry for 10–15 minutes. Serve hot with fresh bread and a salad.

SCALLOPS

A fan-shaped crustacean which has become the trading symbol of the Shell Oil Company. The scallop is also the emblem of Christian pilgrims and has St James as its patron saint. Its reputation among gourmets is equally distinguished and it ranks as one of the world's finest shellfish, having a firm texture and wonderful flavour.

In spite of the relatively high cost of scallops they are becoming more readily available, although it is difficult to find them in their shells unless you order them from a reputable fishmonger. Fresh scallops are at their best in the late winter and early spring but shelled scallops are available all the year round as most are frozen. Fortunately freezing doesn't seem to effect the texture and flavour of scallops too adversely although they are never as good as those straight from the sea.

Scallops have a distinctive flavour which has a special affinity with bacon and mushrooms but, by and large, the simplest ways of cooking them are the best. They are delicious grilled or baked with garlic butter, poached in wine or served *au gratin* with a mornay sauce when they become known by the French name *coquilles St Jacques*.

Allow two large scallops per person or three to four small ones. Like all shellfish scallops cook quickly and care must be taken not to overcook them or they become tough and rubbery.

SCALLOPS COOKED WITH MUSHROOMS AND WINE

I like to serve this dish in individual ramekin pots or empty scallop shells as a first course or starter. It can be prepared in advance and popped in the oven at the last minute.

225g/8 oz shelled scallops
75ml/3 fl. oz dry white wine
50g/2 oz button mushrooms, finely chopped
1 clove of garlic, peeled and crushed
a good pinch of ground mace
seasoning
25g/1 oz soft wholewheat breadcrumbs
15g/½ oz butter

Chop the scallops into bite-sized pieces and put into a small pan. Pour over the wine and bring to a slow boil. Reduce the heat, cover and poach for 1–2 minutes. Drain and reserve the stock. Put the scallops back into the pan along with the mushrooms, garlic and mace. Mix together and season to taste. Spoon the mixture into four individual dishes and spoon 1 tablespoon of cooking stock over each. Sprinkle the breadcrumbs over the top and dot with butter. Bake in a preheated oven, gas mark 8 (230° C/450° F) for 10–12 minutes until the breadcrumbs begin to brown.

SCALLOP AND JERUSALEM ARTICHOKE SOUP

I must thank Margaret Costa for giving me the idea for this soup. The original recipe is to be found in her admirable *Four Seasons Cookery Book* (Sphere, 1972). I have taken the liberty of altering some of the ingredients, making the soup less rich by omitting the cream and egg yolks while emphasising the scallops whose delicate flavour is easily drowned by the more robust artichokes.

2 tbsps sunflower oil
2 onions, chopped
450g/1 lb Jerusalem artichokes, peeled and chopped
1 large potato, peeled and chopped
575ml/1 pint water
225g/8 oz shelled scallops, diced
575ml/1 pint milk

Heat the oil in a large pan, add the onions and sauté for 5–7 minutes until soft and golden. Add the artichokes and the potato, pour over the water and bring to the boil. Cover and simmer gently for 25 minutes until the vegetables are soft. Pass the vegetables and cooking liquid through a vegetable mouli, or process in a liquidiser or food processor. Put the scallops and milk into a pan and bring to the boil. Stir in the puréed vegetables and heat through. Cook gently for a minute or two until the scallops are tender. Season to taste.

SCALLOP, BACON AND MUSHROOM PIE

A lovely combination of flavours, textures and colours makes this one of my favourite pies. For some reason it is evocative of traditional English country cooking. Occasionally I replace some of the milk with dry cider.

350ml/12 fl. oz milk
1 sprig of fresh parsley
1 sprig of fresh thyme
1 bay leaf
½ carrot, sliced
1 slice of onion
6 black peppercorns
175g/6 oz bacon, trimmed and chopped
175g/6 oz flat mushrooms, roughly chopped
175g/6 oz shelled scallops, chopped if large
15g/½ oz butter
1 tbsp sunflower oil
25g/1 oz wholewheat flour

FOR THE PASTRY
175g/6 oz wholewheat self-raising flour
75g/3 oz butter, diced
6 tsps cold water
beaten egg or milk to glaze

Put the milk, herbs, carrot, onion and peppercorns in a pan and bring to the boil. Remove from the heat and leave to stand for 15–20 minutes. Strain and reserve the milk.

Toss the bacon into a frying pan and sauté for 2–3 minutes. Then add the mushrooms and scallops and cook briefly before spooning into a pie dish.

To make the sauce, heat the butter and oil in a pan and stir in the flour. Cook gently for a minute or two until the mixture begins to bubble. Remove from the heat and gradually add the strained milk, stirring well after each addition. Return to the heat and bring to the boil, stirring well, until the sauce thickens. Pour over the bacon, mushrooms and scallops and mix together. Spoon into a pie dish and leave to cool.

To make the pastry, put the flour in a bowl and rub in the butter until the mixture resembles breadcrumbs. Add the water and mix to form a dough. Turn out onto a lightly floured board and roll out. Cover the pie dish, trim the edges and brush with beaten egg or milk. Bake in a preheated oven, gas mark 6 (200° C/400° F), for 25–30 minutes.

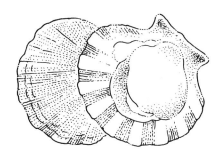

GRILLED SCALLOPS

A first-course dish.

225g/8 oz shelled scallops
15g/½ oz butter

Put the scallops into a shallow ovenproof dish, or better still into four clean scallop shells and dot with butter. Cook under a hot grill for 4–6 minutes until the scallops are meltingly tender. Serve with thin slices of buttered brown bread and wedges of lemon.

SCAMPI, *see* Dublin Bay Prawns

SEA BASS

A fish similar in appearance to the salmon which, presumably, is why it is also known as salmon dace, sea salmon and white salmon. It is covered in silvery scales and is fairly bony. The scales should be removed carefully to avoid tearing the delicate pink skin underneath. The flesh is lean, white and flaky with a good flavour. Small ones can be treated as if they were trout while larger ones can be cooked like salmon.

Available for most of the year, sea bass are rare visitors to the fishmonger's stall. When they do put in an appearance they are sold whole, filleted and as steaks.

SEA BASS WITH TOASTED ALMONDS

4 small sea bass, cleaned
juice of 1 lemon
approx. 75ml/3 fl. oz fish stock (p. 41)
25g/1 oz butter
50g/2 oz flaked almonds
25g/1 oz soft wholewheat breadcrumbs
seasoning

Lay the fish in the bottom of a lightly buttered shallow ovenproof dish. Pour over the lemon juice and fish stock (sufficient to cover the bottom of the dish). Dot with half the butter. Bake in a preheated oven, gas mark 5 (190° C/375° F), for 20 minutes or until tender, basting frequently. Mix the flaked almonds and breadcrumbs together and season to taste. Sprinkle over the fish and dot with the remaining butter. Put under a hot grill to brown.

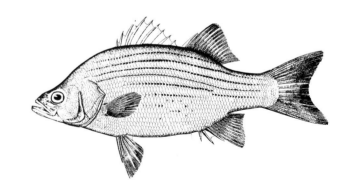

SEA BREAM

A mixed bag of fish comes under the general heading of sea bream. Some, notably the gilt-edged bream, are excellent while others are a little coarse. To confuse matters even further the most common bream on sale in this country, a beautiful orangey-red fish aptly named the red bream, is not a bream at all. Although this may concern marine etymologists it is of little consequence to the average cook for it can be prepared in the same manner as all bream.

Available either whole or filleted, bream are best baked or grilled. If preparing a whole fish for the table leave the head on but remove the rather tough scales. It is a particularly good fish to stuff.

SEA BREAM STUFFED WITH CHESTNUTS

An unusual filling which takes some time to prepare but is well worth the effort. You could cut corners by using dried chestnuts but I don't think the result is as good, as their flavour and texture simply don't compare with those of fresh chestnuts.

225g/8 oz chestnuts
100g/4 oz long grain brown rice
275ml/½ pint water
1–2 tbsps olive oil
2 cloves of garlic, peeled and crushed
100g/4 oz button mushrooms, finely chopped
2 tbsps lemon juice
2 tbsps finely chopped fresh lemon thyme
1 egg, beaten
seasoning
800–900g/1¾–2 lbs sea bream

Make a cut in the outer shell of each chestnut and put them in a pan of water. Bring to the boil, cover and simmer for 20 minutes. Drain and cover the chestnuts with cold water. Taking the nuts from the water, one by one, remove both the hard outer shell and the thinner brown skin. Chop the peeled chestnuts into small pieces and put into a mixing bowl.

While the chestnuts are cooking put the rice in a heavy pan and pour over the water. Bring to the boil, cover and simmer for 35–40 minutes, without stirring, until all the water has been absorbed and the rice is dry and tender. Put into the bowl with the chopped chestnuts. Heat the oil in a frying pan, add the garlic and mushrooms and sauté for 3–4 minutes. Stir this mixture into the bowl and add the lemon juice, lemon thyme and beaten egg. Season to taste.

Scale the fish under cold running water and trim off the fins. Clean, wash carefully and pat dry. Stuff the filling into the fish and brush the skin with olive oil. Wrap the fish in greaseproof paper, *en papillote*, and bake in a preheated oven, gas mark 5 (190° C/375° F), for 35–40 minutes until the fish is tender. Serve with baked potatoes and a green vegetable or salad.

SHRIMPS

There are two types of shrimps on sale in Britain; the pink shrimp which is a fairly common sight around our shores and the less familiar brown shrimp. Look out for the brown ones next time you visit Lancashire, especially around Morecombe Bay and Lytham. They don't look as pretty as their dainty pink cousins but the flavour is much better. All shrimps are best when freshly caught and boiled; they don't freeze as well as the larger prawns.

Shrimps measure less than 5 cm/2 inches from head to tail and are extremely fiddly to peel. With a little practice the head and tail can be gently pulled apart, in such a way that the whole shell comes away in one hand leaving the edible portion attached to the head. They can be served whole, with buttered brown bread and lemon wedges, as a leisurely but delicious starter or tea-time dish.

Potted shrimps is one of our very best regional dishes and I am delighted to see it appearing on the menu of more and more country pubs and hotels. It makes a welcome change from the usual array of ploughman's lunches and things in baskets. Peeled shrimps are also good in sauces, soups, salads and sandwiches and in a smooth, delicately flavoured savoury butter.

POTTED SHRIMPS

100g/4 oz butter
350g/12 oz peeled shrimps
¼–½ tsp ground mace
a pinch of cayenne pepper

Melt the butter in a pan and toss in the shrimps, mace and cayenne pepper. Stir gently and cook for 4–6 minutes over a low heat. Add more spices to taste. Pour into little pots and leave to cool. Cover and leave overnight in a cool place. If the potted shrimps are not to be eaten the next day seal by covering with a thin layer of clarified butter.

SKATE

Skate and ray are members of the same family of flattened cartilaginous fish. Skate is widely used to describe those that are edible while ray is reserved for the fish sporting fishermen catch. However, this doesn't always hold true and some fishmongers hedge their bets by placing two labels, one saying skate and the other ray, on the same batch of fish.

Not so long ago whole skate were not allowed to be carried through the streets in some parts of Britain. They were considered indecent, although I can't imagine why. Skate may not be the most handsome of fish but they are not the sort of creature to produce nightmares. They are, however, fairly unique in that their pectoral fins have grown to such a degree that they are called wings and the whole fish is kite-shaped. Only the wings are eaten, small ones being sold whole while larger ones are cut into pieces. A thick middle cut from a large wing is the best buy as it is easier to prepare and has more meat than smaller pieces.

Skate has no real bones, just pieces of white cartilage. It can be cooked and served whole or 'filleted'. The meat comes away in long, tender strips which can then be served with melted butter or a sauce. If I want to use the bones to make a stock or sauce I usually 'fillet' the skate before cooking it by inserting a sharp knife between the 'bone' and the meat; but it can be done after the skate has been cooked. Dorothy Hartley, in her book *Food in England* (Macdonald, 1964) recommends holding the cooked skate 'with a cloth wrung out in cold water, you'll find you are able to draw out all the bones sideways, like a row of pins'.

Skate is a popular fish for those who detest fish bones and for this reason it is also found heavily disguised in batter, in fish and chip shops throughout the country. As far as its taste and flavour go it has its fair share of admirers and critics. I tend to agree with the lady who said 'when it is good it is very, very good and when it is bad it is awful.' When very fresh, skate smell slightly of ammonia and can be tough. They are best left for a couple of days before being eaten by which time the smell will have disappeared and the meat will be soft and succulent. That doesn't mean to say that they can be left hanging around indefinitely – they go off like any other fish. Most of the skate which appear in our fishmongers have already been 'rested' and need to be eaten straightaway.

Skate are at their best in the autumn and winter. The classic treatment is to poach them in water, to which has been added a dash of vinegar or lemon juice and a slice of onion. The cooked fish is then served with a white sauce and capers or with black butter. *Raie au beurre noir* is a traditional French dish. The butter is heated not, as the name suggests, until it is black but an appetising and attractive nutty brown. While I am sure that chefs on both sides of the Channel are still preparing this dish I do remember hearing that some restaurants have taken it off their menus, the reason being that 'burnt fat' is thought to be a health risk. I wonder if this concern extends to the *pommes frites* pan.

Skate can also be grilled, deep-fried, poached and baked and, because of the gelatinous quality of the carti-lage, it makes good stocks and soups. An excellent dish is skate *au gratin* but the fish also has an affinity with toma-toes. Some gourmets suggest that the liver is a great deli-cacy and, like that of the red mullet, should not be discarded. It is also said to be good spread on hot buttered toast. This may be true but as my skate come skinned, gutted and cut into fan-shaped wedges I have never had the opportunity to put it to the test.

SKATE WITH BEURRE NOIR

2 skate wings, weighing 450g/1 lb each
1 onion, chopped
3 sprigs of fresh parsley
2 tbsps lemon juice
approx. 575ml/1 pint water

FOR THE SAUCE
50g/2 oz butter
1 tsbp white wine vinegar

Put the fish, onion, parsley and lemon juice in a large pan and barely cover with water. Bring to a slow boil, reduce the heat, cover and poach for 8–10 minutes until tender. Lift the fish from the pan with a slotted spoon and leave aside. When cool enough to handle remove the skin and cut each wing into three wedge shaped pieces. Carefully ease the flesh from the cartilaginous bones and arrange it attractively on a serving dish. Cover and keep warm.

To make the sauce, melt the butter in a small pan and cook gently until it becomes golden brown. Pour it over the fish and quickly tip the vinegar into the hot pan where it should bubble and splutter on contact. Pour this over the fish and serve immediately while it is sizzlingly hot. Serve with potatoes or crusty bread and a green salad.

SKATE AU GRATIN

A topping of golden breadcrumbs and sizzling cheese is a simple and delicious way of adding colour, flavour and interest to a dish of baked skate.

1–1.25 kg/2–2¾ lbs skate wings
juice of 1 lemon
275ml/½ pint milk
150ml/¼ pint dry white wine
6 black peppercorns
1 bay leaf
1 slice of onion
1 slice of carrot
15g/½ oz butter
1 tbsp sunflower oil
25g/1 oz unbleached white flour
3–4 tbsps soft wholewheat breadcrumbs
50g/2 oz Cheddar cheese, grated

Trim the skate, slicing through the flesh, as close to the cartilaginous bones as possible, so that it comes away in long strips. Don't worry too much about their shape. Arrange the pieces in the bottom of a shallow ovenproof dish and pour over the lemon juice. Cover with foil and bake in a preheated oven, gas mark 5 (190° C/375° F), for 20 minutes until cooked.

Meanwhile chop what remains of the skate wings and put into a large pan. Add the milk, wine, peppercorns, bay leaf, onion and carrot. Bring to the boil, cover and simmer gently for 15–20 minutes. Strain and reserve the stock. Heat the butter and oil in a pan and stir in the flour. Cook for a minute or two until the mixture begins to bubble. Remove from the heat and gradually add the stock, stirring well after each addition. Return to the heat and cook gently until the sauce begins to thicken. Pour over the cooked fish and sprinkle the breadcrumbs on top. Sprinkle the grated cheese over and put under a hot grill to brown.

SMOKED FISH

British food is rarely the envy of the world but there is one area in which we excel – smoked fish. Our Finnan haddock, Arbroath smokies, smoked salmon and kippers have a reputation second to none. Smoking is a speciality of Northern Europe and it is easy to see why it became both successful and popular here in Britain. Firstly, the necessary raw materials, that is to say abundant supplies of fresh fish and wood shavings, were readily available from harbours and ship-yards dotted around our coasts. Secondly, the numerous meatless days scattered throughout the Christian calendar ensured a large and steady demand, particularly in areas too far from the sea to rely on supplies of fresh fish.

The method of smoking fish has changed little over the centuries but there is reason to believe that today's fish have a better flavour and texture than those of bygone days. This is because with the advent of refrigeration salt and smoke are no longer needed to preserve the fish and can be used in much smaller amounts. Unfortunately refrigeration had also opened the way for a new breed of smoked fish, aptly described by one Scottish kipperer as 'painted ladies'. They are the manufacturers' delight, requiring little skill or time to be mass-produced. Dyed and treated with liquid smoke they masquerade as smokies on many fishmongers' slabs. Luckily there is no mistaking their fierce, bright colours which betray their mock pedigree and they can be avoided easily.

An American writer described the kipper as 'the king of the English breakfast', but I must admit I prefer the Arbroath smokie, a fish which is altogether lighter in flavour and texture, and is much easier on the digestive system.

The budding smoked fish connoisseur should understand one important distinction between the various types. There are two distinct groups: cool or cold smoked; and hot smoked fish. As the name suggests cool smoked fish are smoked at fairly low temperatures and can withstand a certain amount of cooking at home. They may be eaten hot or cold. Smoked salmon, Finnan haddock, kippers and bloaters are all prepared in this way. Hot smoked fish such as smoked trout, mackerel, eel, Arbroath smokies and buckling are subjected to much higher temperatures and are actually cooked during the smoking process. They are usually served cold with slices of brown bread, twists of lemon and salady things but they can be heated through quickly in a hot oven or under a grill. Overcooking can have disastrous consequences as I found to my cost when dealing with my first buckling. Presuming it to be akin to a kipper, I plunged it into a jug of boiling water and when I came to pull it out the whole fish disintegrated.

Whilst I would never say no to a few slices of smoked salmon, my favourite smoked fish is the haddock, sold either as Finnan haddock or Arbroath smokies. It is easy to tell the two apart for Finnan haddock is split open along the belly whereas smokies are not. Both are an attractive tawny brown colour and beneath their glossy golden skin the flesh is soft, moist and delicate. There are many ways of cooking Finnan haddock. It can be grilled or poached, creamed New England style or fried Scottish fashion with ham. It also makes an excellent kedgeree. Arbroath smokies on the other hand require no further cooking and should just be heated through under a hot grill or in a preheated oven and served with a knob of butter and some slices of brown bread. Both fish make very good pâtés.

Some people are deterred from eating smoked fish because many varieties are sold on the bone. This need not be a problem for the backbone can easily be removed, and if handled carefully comes away in one piece. First place the split fish (cool-smoked fish may need to be cooked first) skin downwards on a plate and work the backbone free from the head end. Gently pull the backbone, easing it away from the flesh until it is attached to the tail only. Cut through the bone as close to the tail as possible and discard. Tackling a whole Arbroath smokie is just as simple – lay it on a plate and lift the skin from one side of the fish. Remove or eat the flesh lying on top of the bone then turn it over and do the same on the other side. Treat smoked herrings (bloaters and buckling) in the same way.

Smoked herrings used to be far more common than they are today, bloater paste sandwiches and bloaters on toast being familiar tea-time dishes in Victorian households. Bloaters are traditionally smoked in Yarmouth and they got their name from their rather plump appearance. The fish are not gutted before being smoked and this causes the body to swell up and take on a gamey flavour. They do need gutting, however, before being eaten. Bloaters are so rarely seen in our shops that they have come to be regarded as something of a delicacy, especially when lightly grilled and served with mustard or horseradish sauce.

The most readily available member of the smoked herring family is the kipper. The difference between a genuine oak-smoked kipper and the run-of-the-mill mass-produced varieties, which come filleted and vacuum packed, is enormous. Look out for those from Loch Fyne, Craister and the Isle of Man. Manx food regulations are more stringent than our own and no artificial colouring agents are allowed to be used in the production of their kippers. Available all year round, kippers are best between August and April when they should be fat, firm fleshed and succulent. They can be cooked under a grill, in a hot oven or in a jug of boiling water (see pages 33–34 for directions). I prefer the latter method as it stops the whole house being filled with the smell of cooked kippers, which can, after the initial tantalising whiff, outstay its welcome. Kipper pâté is a good lunch or first course dish (recipe on pages 140–141).

Mackerel, trout, salmon, oysters, cod's roe, mussels and eel can now be bought smoked too. With the exception of smoked mackerel they tend to be rather expensive and are generally eaten with brown bread and lemon juice so that their delicate flavour can be fully appreciated. Pâtés, mousses and terrines are usually made from cheaper scraps and trimmings. One word of caution about smoked salmon – it is important that it is sliced wafer thin. Thick slices may look more substantial but they make dull, heavy eating. I was interested to see in a number of old cookery books that smoked salmon used to be served hot, brushed with butter and then lightly grilled. This certainly isn't the practice today but may be worth trying if you are fortunate enough to have a little smoked salmon to spare.

FINNAN HADDOCK AND PASTA TOSSED WITH YOGHURT

1 tbsp olive oil
350g/12 oz wholewheat pasta shells
approx. 275ml/½ pint milk
500g/1¼ lbs Finnan haddock
4 eggs
275ml/½ pint thick-set natural yoghurt
2–3 tbsps chopped fresh parsley
freshly ground black pepper

Bring a large pan of water to the boil and add the olive oil and pasta. Cook for 10–12 minutes until the pasta is barely tender. Drain well.

Meanwhile cover the bottom of a large pan with about 1.25 cm/½ inch milk, add the fish and bring to a slow boil. Reduce the heat, cover and poach for 4–6 minutes until tender. Remove the fish with a slotted spoon and when cool enough to handle remove the skin and bones. Break the fish into large flakes and put into a shallow ovenproof dish. Add the pasta and mix together carefully. Cover with foil and put into a preheated oven, gas mark 4 (180° C/350° F).

Boil the eggs for 4 minutes and leave to cool. Shell and cut in half. Scoop out the slightly runny yolks and put into a small bowl. Chop the whites and add to the cooked fish and pasta. Bring the milk in which the fish has been cooked to a fast boil and cook until reduced to about 3–4 tablespoons. Pour into the bowl containing the egg yolks. Add the yoghurt and mix together well. Pour the creamy mixture into a pan and heat through, taking care not to let it boil or it may curdle. Stir in the parsley and season to taste. Pour over the fish and pasta and serve.

FINNAN HADDOCK PILAU

1–2 tbsps groundnut oil
1 onion, chopped
1 green pepper, chopped
2 tomatoes, chopped
100g/4 oz button mushrooms, halved if necessary
100g/4 oz sweetcorn
450g/1 lb Finnan haddock, lightly poached and drained
225g/8 oz long grain brown rice, cooked seasoning

Heat the oil in a heavy pan, add the onion and sauté for 5–7 minutes until soft and golden. Stir in the green pepper and cook for 5 minutes more. Add the tomatoes, mushrooms and sweetcorn and stir-fry for several minutes more. Flake the fish, removing the skin and as many bones as possible. Put into the vegetable pan along with the cooked rice. Season to taste. Spoon into an ovenproof dish, cover and heat through in a preheated oven, gas mark 6 (200° C/400° F), for 15–20 minutes.

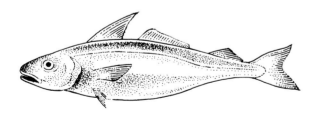

GOLDEN HADDOCK PIE

150ml/¼ pint milk
1 slice of onion
½ leek, sliced
6 black peppercorns
1 bay leaf
225g/8 oz haddock fillets
225g/8 oz smoked haddock fillets
2 hard-boiled eggs
50g/2 oz frozen peas
2 tbsps finely chopped fresh parsley
freshly ground black pepper
25g/1 oz butter
20g/¾ oz unbleached white flour
freshly grated nutmeg
675–900g/1½–2 lbs cooked potatoes, mashed

Put the milk, onion, leek, peppercorns, bay leaf and fish in a large pan. Bring to a slow boil, reduce the heat, cover and poach for 4–6 minutes until tender. Carefully lift the fish from the pan and when cool enough to handle remove the skin and any bones. Flake the fish into a bowl. Chop the hard-boiled eggs and add to the flaked fish. Stir in the peas and parsley and season with black pepper. Strain the milk and reserve until needed.

Melt the butter in a pan and stir in the flour. Cook gently for a minute or two, stirring occasionally and then remove from the heat. Gradually add the strained milk, stirring well after each addition. Return to the heat and bring to the boil, stirring well, until the sauce thickens. Season with nutmeg. Pour over the fish and vegetables and mix together. Spoon into a pie dish and cover with mashed potatoes. Bake in a preheated oven, gas mark 5 (190° C/375° F), for 20 minutes. To brown the potatoes put under a hot grill for 5–6 minutes.

KEDGEREE

Kedgeree was brought back to England from India by the colonials. Originally it consisted of curried fish and rice served with hard-boiled eggs but English cooks have modified the ingredients over the years and few kedgerees now contain any curry spices. I add lots of vegetables to my kedgeree and the overall effect is both mouth-watering and colourful. If you like, stir in a little single cream before serving.

1–2 tbsps olive oil
1 red pepper, chopped
275g/10 oz long grain rice
100g/4 oz button mushrooms, halved if necessary
100g/4 oz frozen peas   100g/4 oz sweetcorn
725ml/1¼ pints water
225g/8 oz Finnan haddock
225g/8 oz haddock fillets
butter
4 hard-boiled eggs, chopped   seasoning

Heat the oil in a heavy pan, add the red pepper and rice and sauté for 3–4 minutes until the rice begins to look translucent. Add the mushrooms, peas and sweetcorn and pour in the water. Bring to the boil, cover and simmer until the rice is tender. Drain if necessary.

While the rice is cooking, brush the fish with a knob of melted butter and put under a hot grill for several minutes until tender. Remove and when cool enough to handle remove the skin and bones. Break into large flakes and stir into the cooked rice. Add the hard-boiled eggs and season to taste. Dot with about 25g/1 oz more butter, if you like. Then, if necessary, cover and heat through in a moderate oven.

SMOKED HADDOCK AND MACARONI AU GRATIN

500g/1¼ lbs Finnan haddock
575ml/1 pint milk
225g/8 oz wholewheat macaroni
50g/2 oz frozen peas
50g/2 oz frozen sweetcorn
1 small cauliflower, broken into pieces
1 baking apple, peeled and chopped
seasoning
50g/2 oz butter
50g/2 oz unbleached white flour
freshly grated nutmeg
50g/2 oz Cheddar cheese, grated

Put the fish in a pan and barely cover with milk. Bring to a slow boil, reduce the heat, cover and poach for 4–6 minutes until tender. Drain and reserve the stock. When the fish is cool enough to handle remove the skin and as many of the bones as possible. Break into large flakes and keep aside until needed.

Bring a large pan of water to the boil and add the macaroni. Cook for 4 minutes and then add the peas, sweetcorn and cauliflower. Cook for a further 5–6 minutes until the pasta and vegetables are just tender. Drain well. Return the pasta and vegetables to the pan. Stir in the flaked fish and chopped apple. Season to taste and spoon into an ovenproof dish.

Melt the butter in a pan, stir in the flour and cook for a minute or two, letting the mixture bubble. Remove from the heat and gradually add the reserved milk, stirring well after each addition. Return to the heat and bring to the boil, stirring frequently, until the sauce begins to thicken. Thin down with a little more milk if necessary. Season to taste with nutmeg. Pour over the other ingredients and mix together well. Sprinkle the grated cheese on top. Warm through in a preheated oven, gas mark 6 (200° C/400° F), or under a hot grill until the cheese topping has begun to brown and the sauce is hot and bubbling.

KIPPER FLAN

175g/6 oz wholewheat flour
75g/3 oz butter, diced
6 tsps cold water

FOR THE FILLING
1 large kipper
225ml/8 fl. oz natural yoghurt or soured cream
3 eggs
1–2 tsps Dijon mustard
freshly ground black pepper

Put the flour in a bowl and rub in the butter until the mixture resembles breadcrumbs. Add the cold water and mix to form a dough. Roll out the pastry on a lightly floured board and line a 20 cm/8 inch flan ring. Prick the base with a fork and blind bake in a preheated oven, gas mark 6 (200° C/400° F), for 10 minutes.

Meanwhile drop the kipper, head first, into a jug of boiling water. Leave to stand for 4–6 minutes. Drain well and when cool remove the skin and bones. Chop the fish and arrange in the bottom of the pastry case. Beat the yoghurt, eggs and mustard together and season to taste. Pour over the kipper and return to the oven. Bake for 25 minutes until firm to the touch and lightly browned.

MARINATED KIPPERS

Serves 4 as a first course or starter
2 boned kipper fillets
1 shallot, finely chopped
2 tbsps sunflower oil
2 tbsps dry white wine
a good pinch of chilli powder

Skin the kippers and cut into strips, then place in a shallow bowl. Mix all the remaining ingredients together and pour over the kippers. Cover and leave to stand in a cool place or refrigerator overnight. Drain well and serve with brown bread.

KIPPER SCRAMBLE

Serves 2–3
1 kipper
a knob of butter
4 eggs, beaten
freshly ground black pepper

Drop the kipper, head first, into a jug of boiling water. Leave to stand for 4–6 minutes, then lift out and drain well. Remove the skin and bones, and keep warm until needed. Melt the butter in a small pan and add the eggs. Stir occasionally until lightly cooked. Gently mix in the flaked kipper and season with black pepper. Spoon over buttered brown toast before taking to the table.

SMOKED MUSSELS COOKED IN GARLIC BUTTER

Smoked fish have become increasingly popular in recent years and such delicacies as smoked trout, smoked eel and smoked cod's roe are to be found on the menus of fashionable restaurants. Imagine my surprise when I came across a small country hotel in Shropshire serving smoked mussels. I love mussels and the idea of eating them smoked was too good an opportunity to miss. They arrived at the table swimming in a hot sizzling bath of golden garlic butter looking disarmingly like any other mussel but after the first delicious mouthful one was left in no doubt that these mussels were special. Both their flavour and texture seemed to be improved by smoking, lifting them into a class of their own.

4 cloves of garlic, peeled and crushed
75g/3 oz soft butter
1 tbsp finely chopped fresh parsley
450g/1 lb shelled smoked mussels

Cream the garlic and butter together. Stir in the parsley. Arrange the mussels in the bottom of an *au gratin* dish and dot small, hazelnut-sized pieces of garlic butter over the top. Put under a hot grill and cook until the butter sizzles. Serve immediately with triangles of wholewheat toast and lemon wedges.

FISH PÂTÉ (1)

Smoked mackerel is fast becoming a most popular cold fish dish and is served, adorned with limp lettuce, tomato and cucumber, at most salad bars throughout the summer. I much prefer it made into creamy pâtés, a number of which are described below (they can also be made with other smoked fish, such as smoked trout, kippers and Arbroath smokies).

225g/8 oz smoked fish, skinned and boned
100g/4 oz natural cottage cheese
1 level tsp horseradish sauce
juice of ½ lemon
seasoning

Pass the fish through the coarse plate of a vegetable mouli or a food processor. It can be pounded in a pestle and mortar but this is hard work. Put the fish into a bowl. Rub the cottage cheese through a sieve into the bowl. Stir in the remaining ingredients and season to taste. Press the mixture into a pâté dish, cover and leave in the refrigerator for several hours to firm up. Serve with brown bread and butter or toasted fingers.

If the pâté is to be kept for more than 24 hours seal the top with clarified butter.

FISH PÂTÉ (2)

225g/8 oz smoked fish, skinned and boned
100g/4 oz curd cheese
1 level tsp tomato purée
½ tsp paprika
juice of ½ lemon
seasoning

Prepare as above, but there is no need to sieve the curd cheese.

FISH PÂTÉ (3)

225g/8 oz smoked fish, skinned and boned
100g/4 oz low-fat cream cheese
juice of ½ lemon
1 tbsp finely chopped fresh chives
seasoning

Prepare as above, but there is no need to sieve the cheese.

SNAPPER

A pinkish-grey fish which lives off the Gulf coasts of America but is increasingly to be found in our fish-mongers' shops. Although only available in this country deep-frozen, small whole snappers are worth buying. They are best grilled or baked and are particularly good served with a hot, spicy tomato sauce.

SPRATS

Sprats are attractive silvery fish, slightly larger and chubbier than whitebait. They grow up to 15 cm/6 inches in length but those on sale in the shops are usually much smaller. Like herrings and sardines they are best grilled or dry-fried and are delicious eaten with brown bread and lemon wedges.

Although sprats are abundant in our seas and are therefore relatively cheap, we don't make full use of them and a large proportion of our catch is exported to Norway only to be re-imported, at twice the price, as tinned brisling. Perhaps the surplus could be put to better use if we took up the idea mooted in *Kettner's Book of the Table*: 'Some time since C—— went to visit a friend in the country who had the most marvellous roses in full bloom. Every one exclaimed at their beauty, and asked "How do you get such?" The gentleman who owned them was a man of few words, and only said "Sprats". It seemed that he manured them with loads of stinking sprats. Not long afterwards a man called at my house with sprats. "Are they stinking?" said I eagerly. "No," said the man, "quite fresh." "Then bring me the first stinking ones you have." In a few days he came with a heavy heart, and offered me a large quantity which had turned putrid on his hands. The result was that on a very small bush I had thirty-six blossoms all at once of magnificent Marshal Niels.'

Small sprats can be cooked like whitebait, indeed if they are small enough they will be sold as whitebait. Larger ones need gutting. I also remove their heads and backbones, taking the viscera with them, otherwise the experience of eating them whole becomes a little too crunchy for comfort. Full-sized sprats can be cooked as if they were herrings and may even need scaling.

DRY-FRIED SPRATS

Wash and dry 450g/1 lb sprats carefully. Heat a heavy frying pan and then add the fish, a few at a time, making sure that each sprat is touching the bottom of the pan. Cook over a moderately hot heat until the sprats begin to brown, turn over and cook the other side likewise. Remove from the pan and keep warm while cooking the remaining fish.

Serve as a light lunch or supper dish with fresh bread and lemon wedges.

SQUID

Squid are torpedo-shaped cephalopods with a cluster of tentacles at one end and two triangular fins at the other. Right through the centre of the sac-like body is a transparent quill which is removed, along with the head and viscera, before cooking. As a rule only the fleshy body, the tentacles and fins are used in recipes, the rest being discarded during the initial cleaning. A step by step guide showing how to clean and prepare squid is shown on page 25. Like all cephalopods squid contain ink sacs which are used in some recipes to colour and flavour sauces but normally these too are discarded.

Squid vary in length but only those measuring between 10–60 cm/4–12 inches find their way into our shops. Generally speaking the smaller the squid the more tender it will be. Very small squid (*calamaretti*), often no more than 3.75 cm/1½ inches long, can be floured or battered and then deep-fried. They are delicious eaten with fresh bread and lemon wedges. Larger squid are usually cut up (I slice the body into 6 mm/¼ inch rings) and when cooked properly are as tender as their smaller siblings. They can be blanched and deep-fried or gently stewed for 35–50 minutes with olive oil, tomatoes, onions, garlic, parsley, celery, red wine and a little water. When cooking squid it is important to understand the basic principle that the larger the squid the longer it will take to cook.

Another excellent way of preparing squid is to stuff the empty body sac with all manner of savoury fillings. Choose squid with bodies measuring between 10–15 cm/4–6 inches long, which are ideally shaped for the purpose. Chop the tentacles and fins and sauté them in oil before incorporating them with the stuffing ingredients.

SQUID COOKED IN RED WINE

A delicious stew with a Mediterranean flavour.

675g/1½ lbs squid
2–3 tbsps olive oil
3 large leeks, sliced
1 small onion, sliced
2 cloves of garlic, peeled and crushed
450g/1 lb tomatoes, diced
425ml/¾ pint red wine
150ml/¼ pint water
2 tbsps chopped fresh parsley
1 tbsp chopped fresh thyme

Prepare the squid as shown on page 25. Chop the tentacles and fins and slice the body into 6 mm/¼ inch rings.

Heat the oil in a heavy pan and add the leeks, onion and garlic. Sauté for 5–7 minutes until soft and golden. Toss in the squid and cook for a further 4–5 minutes, stirring frequently. Add the remaining ingredients and season to taste. Cover and bring to the boil. Simmer gently for 35–50 minutes until the squid is tender. Serve with brown rice or potatoes.

SQUID COOKED WITH FRESH GINGER

A delicately flavoured fish curry.

675g/1½ lbs squid
1 small cauliflower
1–2 tbsps groundnut oil
1 onion, sliced
5 cm/2 inch fresh root ginger, peeled and grated
2 tsps ground coriander
1 tsp turmeric
1 potato, diced
approx. 425ml/¾ pint water
2–3 tbsps finely chopped fresh coriander

Prepare the squid as shown on page 25. Slice into thin rings and chop the tentacles and fins. Cut the cauliflower into bite-sized pieces.

Heat the oil in a pan, add the onion and sauté for 5–7 minutes. Add the ginger, coriander and turmeric and stir-fry for 1–2 minutes. Next toss in the squid and potato and pour over the water. Bring to the boil, cover and simmer gently for 10–15 minutes. Stir well to thicken the curry and sprinkle with fresh coriander. Serve with brown rice or chapati.

SICILIAN STUFFED SQUID

The delicate, creamy-coloured squid is an ideal vehicle for all kinds of savoury stuffings. I particularly like this one as the flavour and texture of the rice, pine kernels and Parmesan cheese complement those of the squid beautifully. However, there is no reason why other fillings shouldn't taste just as delicious, particularly those already put to good use in such dishes as stuffed tomatoes, stuffed courgettes and stuffed peppers.

8–10 squid (their bodies measuring 10–15 cm/4–6 inches long)
1–2 tbsps olive oil
1 onion, chopped
100g/4 oz long grain brown rice
275ml/½ pint water
2–3 tbsps finely chopped fresh parsley
50g/2 oz pine kernels
5–6 tbsps Parmesan cheese, grated
freshly ground black pepper
75g/3 oz soft wholewheat breadcrumbs

Prepare the squid as shown on page 25. Chop the tentacles and fins into small pieces but leave the pouch-like bodies whole.

Heat the oil in a heavy pan, add the onion and sauté for 5–7 minutes. Then add the chopped squid and the rice. Cook for a further 3–4 minutes, stirring frequently, until the rice becomes slightly translucent. Pour over the water and bring to the boil. Cover and simmer for 35–40 minutes, without stirring, until all the water has been absorbed and the rice is dry and tender. Stir in the parsley, pine kernels and 2–3 tablespoons of the Parmesan cheese. Season to taste with black pepper.

Stuff the squid loosely with the filling mixture; if packed too tightly the squid may burst open during cooking. Arrange in the bottom of a lightly oiled ovenproof dish. Mix the breadcrumbs and the remaining cheese together in a small bowl and then sprinkle over the squid. Bake in a preheated oven, gas mark 4 (180° C/350° F), for 40–60 minutes until the squid is tender.

TROUT

Up until the 1950s everyone in England ate trout whenever they could, and country rectories, mountain farms and lakeside inns produced trout for breakfast. At least that is what Dorothy Hartley says in *Food in England* (Macdonald 1964). Perhaps this was true in the Yorkshire Dales where she was brought up but I certainly don't remember seeing many trout in my home town, situated as it was on the border between Yorkshire and Lincolnshire. I don't think I even ate one until I went away to college. Then I would order trout and almonds at bistro-style restaurants and feel very sophisticated.

Since then there has been something of a trout boom and they can now be found all the year round in almost every town. Though this is good news to the non-angling fish lover there is, as always, a slight catch. Most of the trout on sale today are bred in tanks and ponds specifically for the table. Their colour and flavour are dependent upon what they are given to eat, and regrettably some have about as much culinary interest as a white sliced loaf. Although I no longer go out of my way to order trout in restaurants I still enjoy eating them, provided that they are very fresh. If this is the case it often doesn't matter whether they have come from a fish farm, stream or reservoir.

In France, where food is taken much more seriously than here in Britain, many restaurants have their own small tanks from which customers can select their own fish. They are killed immediately prior to being cooked. I presume this is why *truite au bleu* features regularly on French menus but not on our own, for in order for the dish to be successful the fish must be poached within minutes of being killed. If left any longer it will not turn the delectable, smoky blue colour which is the hallmark of this famous dish.

On one occasion while holidaying in the South of France I watched as the tranquillity of a village square was broken by the hooting of a small van as it drew up alongside the fountain. Men, women and children appeared from behind shuttered windows, laughing and gesticulating to one another. Within a few minutes sleek shimmering live trout were being fished out of the tank on the back of the van for the customers. Before driving off, the fishman tossed a couple of fat trout into the small pool beneath the fountain. They were still swimming in the dappled waters when I had finished my coffee and I was sorely tempted to fish one out and take it back for supper.

Of the three common European trout, the rainbow trout is the one most likely to be found on a fish farm. It can survive stagnant water conditions much better than the brown trout. Generally the brown trout is said to have the better flavour but again it depends on what the fish have been eating. I have had some very indifferent brown trout, and large lake trout are reputed to be dry, tough and lacking in flavour.

Rainbow trout and brown trout are sold whole, usually weighing on average between 175–225g/6–8 oz which is an ideal size for one person. They have a delicate flavour and need to be accompanied by subtle, light ingredients. A really fresh trout needs nothing more than a little melted butter or a *beurre blanc* sauce. Both these trout can be poached, grilled, baked, cooked *en papillote* or fried.

Gut the fish through the gills or the belly. When stuffing a trout it is best to cut it open along the back and to remove the backbone and guts from the top. The gills should be pushed from their slits and removed. It is usual to leave the heads intact and many cooks also leave the eyes in situ as they are a useful cooking guide, for when they turn quite white the fish is done. They can then be removed with the point of a knife and a sprig of parsley put in their place before serving. If you want to remove the skin do so after the fish has been cooked.

Just as the salmon trout is challenging the salmon in high culinary circles so a similar rivalry exists between smoked trout and smoked salmon. In this matter I must confess to being on the side of the salmon but that is not to say that I don't enjoy a dish of smoked trout pâté (recipe on pages 140–141). Smoked trout is also good filleted and served with thin slices of brown bread and lemon wedges. Personally I don't much like the current vogue of serving horseradish sauce with it – I don't think that the delicate, smoky flavour of the fish can stand up against such a fierce onslaught.

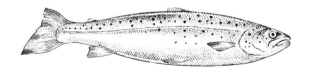

TROUT WITH OATMEAL

4 trout
a little milk
some medium oatmeal
freshly ground black pepper
50g/2 oz unsalted butter

Clean the fish and remove their heads and tails. Carefully fillet them, leaving the skins on. Dip in milk. Season some oatmeal with black pepper and sprinkle over the fish. Fry in butter until well browned on both sides.

For a healthier and more economical dish omit the butter and dry-fry the fish in a preheated heavy frying pan.

GRILLED TROUT WITH MUSHROOMS

4 trout, trimmed and cleaned
butter
100g/4 oz button mushrooms, thinly sliced
1–2 tbsps finely chopped fresh parsley
juice of ½ lemon

Make two to three diagonal cuts in both sides of each fish. Brush with melted butter and cook under a hot grill. Meanwhile melt another knob of butter in a small pan and sauté the mushrooms for 2–3 minutes. Stir in the parsley and add a dash of lemon juice to taste. Spoon over the cooked trout and serve immediately.

BAKED TROUT WITH MUSHROOM AND HAZELNUT STUFFING

4 trout
1–2 tbsps olive oil
225g/8 oz button mushrooms, chopped
75g/3 oz roasted hazelnuts, chopped
2–3 tbsps finely chopped fresh thyme
seasoning

Trim the fish and remove the backbone and guts from an opening along the back. Remove the gills. Rinse well and pat dry.

Heat the oil in a frying pan, add the mushrooms and sauté for several minutes. Add the remaining ingredients and season to taste. Stuff the mixture into the cleaned fish. Place each trout on a piece of oiled foil or greaseproof paper and fold, *en papillote*, to make four loose parcels. Bake in a preheated oven, gas mark 5 (190° C/375° F) for 20–25 minutes.

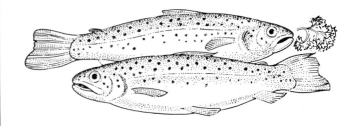

STUFFED TROUT EN CROÛTE

Each trout is filled with roasted almonds and raisins before being sealed inside a pastry case. It's great fun shaping the pastry to look like a fish, giving it a mouth, tail, fins, eyes etc. Although it is something of a time-consuming job it never fails to impress and amuse friends and guests. I serve it hot or cold with new potatoes, a vegetable and béchamel sauce.

4 small trout
100g/4 oz split almonds, lightly roasted
100g/4 oz raisins
seasoning

FOR THE PASTRY
450g/1 lb wholewheat flour
225g/8 oz butter, diced
5–6 tbsps cold water
1 egg, beaten, to glaze

Trim each fish and remove the backbone and guts from an opening along the back. Remove the gills. Rinse well and pat dry. Mix the almonds and raisins together and season to taste. Stuff the mixture into each cleaned trout. Place aside until needed.

To make the pastry, put the flour in a bowl and rub in the butter until the mixture resembles breadcrumbs. Add the water and mix to form a dough. Divide the dough into eight equal parts. Place two pieces on a floured board and roll out into oblongs, slightly larger that the fish. Lay a trout on one of the oblongs and cut round it leaving a good 1.25 cm/½ inch margin. Cut the other piece of pastry to a similar shape. Cover the trout. Dampen the pastry edges with water and press together to seal. Trim away any surplus pastry. Use the pastry trimmings to make the eyes and fins. Make a mark behind the eye to represent the gills and score the tail and fins. If you have the time and patience mark on the scales but remember that there are still three more fish to wrap up!

When all the trout are sealed inside their pastry cases place on an oiled baking tray and brush with beaten egg. Bake in a preheated oven, gas mark 5 (190° C/375° F), for 25–30 minutes.

POACHED TROUT

If you are fortunate enough to have several small, fresh trout try cooking them in a light, delicate court-bouillon. I suggest that you also add to the pan a little well-flavoured fumet or fish stock, a sprig or two of parsley, a whole clove, a slice of onion and a glass of dry white wine. Poach the fish for 5–8 minutes until tender. Carefully lift from the pan, drain and arrange on a serving dish. Serve with a *beurre blanc* sauce or melted butter.

BAKED TROUT WITH SOURED CREAM AND CUCUMBER

Being fairly health- and weight-conscious I rarely cook with cream but I am quite happy to make an exception with this dish. It is, I think, one of the nicest ways of eating trout.

4 trout
25g/1 oz butter
juice of 1 lemon
2 tbsps finely chopped fresh parsley
½ cucumber
275ml/½ pint soured cream

Clean and trim the fish, leaving their heads and tails in place. Remove the gills.

Melt the butter in a small pan and brush a little over a shallow ovenproof dish. Lay the fish in the bottom, pour over the lemon juice and sprinkle with parsley. Cover with a piece of buttered foil. Bake in a preheated oven, gas mark 5 (190° C/375° F), for 15 minutes. Meanwhile peel the cucumber and cut into julienne strips (shaped like matchsticks). Heat what remains of the melted butter and toss in the cucumber. Sauté for 3–4 minutes and then pour in the soured cream. Heat through gently.

Remove the foil from the fish and pour over the soured cream and cucumber mixture. Replace the foil and bake for a further 5–10 minutes until the trout are tender. Serve with new potatoes and a salad.

TUNA

Tunny or tuna is a member of the herring family and grows to an enormous size. It is occasionally seen off the Cornish coast but its real homeland is in the Mediterranean and the warm seas of the mid Atlantic. It is seldom sold fresh in this country but should you be lucky enough to come across it the steaks are excellent grilled, barbecued or stewed with tomatoes, peppers and olives. The meat is rich, firm textured and oily.

TUNNY À LA PROVENÇALE

A colourful dish in which the acidity of the tomatoes and lemon juice counteracts the richness of the fish.

2 tbsps olive oil
2 onions, chopped
2 cloves of garlic, peeled and crushed
1 large red pepper, sliced
450g/1 lb ripe tomatoes, chopped
juice of 2 lemons
12 black olives, stoned
500g/1¼ lbs tuna fish steaks
seasoning

Heat the oil in a heavy pan, add the onions and garlic and sauté for 5–7 minutes. Add the red pepper, tomatoes, lemon juice and olives, then cover and simmer gently until the tomatoes have softened. Chop the fish into bite-sized pieces, removing the skin and as many of the bones as possible. Put into the pan with the other ingredients. Cover and cook gently for a further 15–20 minutes until tender. Season to taste.

TURBOT

Turbot has always been regarded as one of the finest sea fish. The Victorians and Edwardians were particularly fond of it, appreciating the lean, white, firm, well-flavoured meat and, if we are to believe Jenny Wren (*Modern Domestic Cookery*, 1880) and Mrs Beeton the turbot's fins were regarded as something of a delicacy. Mrs Wren gives strict instructions that the cook should not tamper with the fins, which are the 'tid-bit' of the turbot, while Mrs Beeton says that when a turbot is served it is polite to ask the guests if they are 'fin fanciers' or not.

The fish served at Victorian and Edwardian tables would have been enormous specimens, by modern standards, for the turbot is one of the largest flat fish and when fully grown can weigh up to 12 kg/26½ lbs. In those days it was customary to cook the fish whole, in a huge diamond-shaped fish kettle known as a turbotière. Nowadays there is little demand for such large fish, and turbot is generally sold in fillets or steaks. Whole baby turbot or chicken turbot, weighing between 900g–2kg/ 2–4½ lbs, are sometimes available and are ideal for large family gatherings or dinner parties. Choose fish which is creamy white, firm and flaky; any hint of blueness to fish is a sure sign that it is past its best.

It is easy to recognise a turbot for its brown skin is very knobbly. One is generally advised, before poaching a whole fish, to make an incision down the backbone on the dark side. This will ensure that the white underbelly does not split open during cooking. Turbot should be available all year round but I doubt whether you will see them at the fishmonger's all that often and even then you will have to pay dearly for the pleasure of eating this fine fish.

Turbot can be baked, poached, steamed or grilled; largish pieces are best wrapped in foil and baked in a moderate oven. The traditional accompaniments are shrimp, oyster or lobster sauce; but parsley or egg sauce and melted butter also complement rather than compete with the fish's excellent flavour.

TURBOT BAKED WITH YOGHURT

675g/1½ lbs turbot fillets, skinned if necessary
275ml/½ pint natural yoghurt
1 egg yolk
juice of 1 orange
freshly grated nutmeg
seasoning
50g/2 oz soft wholewheat breadcrumbs
15g/½ oz butter

Place the fillets in a lightly buttered ovenproof dish. Beat the yoghurt, egg yolk and orange juice together. Add a little freshly grated nutmeg and season to taste. Pour the mixture over the fish. Sprinkle the breadcrumbs on top and dot with butter. Bake in a preheated oven, gas mark 5 (190° C/375° F), for 25–30 minutes until the fish is tender. If necessary, raise the oven temperature to gas mark 8 (230° C/450° F) and continue to cook for 5–7 minutes until the breadcrumbs become golden, or brown under a hot grill.

WHELKS AND WINKLES

Both whelks and winkles are sold, by and large, ready boiled and are perhaps more commonly thought of as a seafood snack to be enjoyed while strolling along the promenade. However, in some parts of northern England they are served up with bread and butter for tea.

WHITEBAIT

Less than a hundred years ago huge shoals of whitebait were being caught in the Thames during the summer and it was fashionable to go to the taverns and public houses at Greenwich and Blackwall for whitebait dinners which were eaten with iced champagne or punch. Even Cabinet Ministers indulged themselves once a year, either at The Trafalgar Tavern or The Ship in Greenwich; at least they did so until 1895 when Gladstone put a stop to such frivolities. Sadly the custom has never been revived, sadly being the operative word, for I agree with W.M. Thackeray who said of whitebait, 'that little means of obtaining a great pleasure'. I am pleased to report, however, that the Whitebait Festival held annually at Southend-on-Sea is still flourishing.

Whitebait can still be brought fresh at towns on the east and south coasts but most are deep frozen as soon as they are caught. Frozen whitebait, although not quite in the same league as those sold fresh, are nonetheless excellent value and well worth eating. They have the advantage of being available all year round.

Whitebait are the offspring or parr of the common herring and sprat, being caught and sold when less than 5 cm/2 inches long. They are so tiny that it is both futile and unnecessary to gut them. However, be wary of the slightly larger sprat whose head and bones are better developed. Whitebait are generally deep-fried before being served with brown bread and butter and lemon wedges (see page 36 for method). When served with a liberal sprinkling of cayenne pepper they are known as devilled whitebait. Allow 100g/4 oz per person.

If you don't like deep-frying food, dry-fry the whitebait in a hot, heavy frying pan (see page 36 for method).

BATTERED WHITEBAIT

25g/1 oz unbleached white flour
1 egg
150–175ml/5–6 fl. oz milk
seasoning
450g/1 lb whitebait
additional flour

Beat the flour, egg and most of the milk together until smooth. Add the remaining milk gradually until the mixture has the consistency of thick cream. Season well.

Wash the whitebait and pat dry with a cloth. Dust with a little additional flour and dip into the batter. Deep-fry, a handful at a time, in hot fat for 3–4 minutes. Put into a dish lined with absorbent paper and keep warm until all the fish have been cooked. Serve with brown bread and lemon wedges.

WHITING

Whiting are still plentiful in the North Sea and are available at a reasonable price throughout the year, although they are at their best between November and March. They are related to the cod and have a similarly tarnished culinary reputation. In the hands of a bad cook their large, delicately flavoured sweet-tasting flakes can be made to look like a ragged dish cloth – overcooking is usually the culprit. This is unfortunate for fresh whiting can be delicious and merit much better treatment. They can be grilled, or fried, cooked like Dover sole or plaice or used to make excellent soufflés or quenelles (dainty fish dumplings lightly poached in stock).

Most whiting are sold filleted today but not so long ago it was fashionable to serve whole fish in the French style (*merlan en colère*). The fish was curled into a ring with its tail secured in its mouth or pushed through the eye sockets. It must have been a fine sight when carried to the table but it is not the best way to cook a fish. It is almost impossible to cook it evenly – what happens is that the flesh on the outside cooks more quickly than that concertina-ed in the middle. Faced with this dilemma the cook has two options – to serve the fish with the middle part underdone or to wait for a few minutes by which time the outside will be overcooked. Neither option is satisfactory as far as the diner is concerned. Occasionally I do buy whole fish but only because they are useful for thickening and enriching fish soups and stews.

WHITING AU GRATIN

1 tbsp sunflower oil
6 shallots, finely chopped
225g/8 oz button mushrooms, sliced
seasoning
2–3 tbsps dry white wine
450g/1 lb whiting fillets
75–100g/3–4 oz soft wholewheat breadcrumbs
25–50g/1–2 oz butter
2–3 tbsps grated Parmesan cheese

Heat the oil in a pan, add the shallots and sauté for several minutes. Add the mushrooms and cook for 1–2 minutes more. Season to taste and moisten with the wine. Spoon into a shallow ovenproof dish and lay the fillets on top. Cover with breadcrumbs, dot with butter and sprinkle over the Parmesan. Bake in a preheated oven, gas mark 6 (200° C/400° F) for 15–20 minutes until lightly browned.

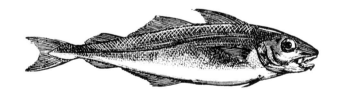

GOLDEN WHITING

A traditional Cornish dish.

approx. 275ml/½ pint fish stock (p. 41)
a pinch of saffron strands
2 large carrots, finely chopped
1 tbsp sunflower oil
2 onions, finely chopped
a pinch of dried mixed herbs
seasoning
450g/1 lb whiting fillets

Put the fish stock in a small pan, add the saffron and bring to the boil. Simmer gently for 10 minutes. Meanwhile parboil the carrots and then drain.

Heat the oil in a frying pan, add the onions and sauté for 5–7 minutes until they begin to soften. Remove from the heat before stirring in the carrots, mixed herbs and seasoning. Chop the fish into large pieces and arrange in the bottom of an ovenproof dish. Spoon over the vegetable mixture and barely cover with saffron stock. Bake in a preheated oven, gas mark 5 (190° C/375° F) for 15–20 minutes. Serve with potatoes.

WRASSE

The most common wrasse found off our shores is of moderate size, measuring up to 50 cm/20 inches, and has a dappled complexion of greens and browns. Although some cooks suggest poaching or steaming wrasse this is not a common practice and it is best used to add flavour and body to soups and stews.

INDEX

N7